The Query

What is the reason for the hope that is within you?

Larry Moeller

Prepare to eavesdrop on conversations with random strangers across America as they answer this simple question – and discover its power as the path to a cultural course correction grounded in hope:
The Reshaping of America, One Query at a Time.

Parson's Porch Books

The Query: "*What is the reason for the hope that is within you?*"
ISBN 9781949888997
Copyright © 2016 by Larry D. Moeller. All rights reserved.

No portion of this publication may be reproduced, stored in a retrieval system, or transmitted in any form or by any means – electronic, mechanical, photocopy, recording, scanning, or other – except for brief quotations in critical reviews or articles, without the prior written permission of the author.

Unless otherwise designated, Scripture quotations are taken from the *HOLY BIBLE: NEW INTERNATIONAL VERSION*®. © 1973, 1978, 1984 by International Bible Society. Used by permission of Zondervan Publishing House. All rights reserved.

NAB. When designated as NAB, the Scripture quotations contained herein are from *The New American Bible*, World Catholic Press, a Division of Catholic Book Publishing Corp., Totowa NJ ©1987. All rights reserved.

NRSV. When designated as NRSV, the Scripture quotations contained herein are from the *New Revised Standard Version Bible*, copyright 1989, by the Division of Christian Education of the National Council of Churches of Christ in the U.S.A. Used by permission. All rights reserved.

Parson's Porch Books
423-475-7308
www.parsonporchbooks.com

Early Commentary on *The Query*

From Some Who Shared Their Stories

Frank. *I appreciate the way you captured the hopes, fears and dreams of all … you put humanity across a stranger's face. There is a sense of Ernie Pyle to it all, with a spiritual twist and a bit of Studs Terkel. I finally got to my story and recalled the conversation like it was yesterday. You were able to take the droll and make it interesting.* [Critical Analysis]

Ignacio. *I like the spirit and style that you have chosen for your 'Queries'. One feels the 'extemporarity' of them, which draws the interest of the reader for the spontaneity of the stories. THANK YOU. You have been very substantially faithful to my story. To tell the truth, I had forgotten many particulars of that 'aerial' encounter, and I thank you for giving me the opportunity of refreshing the memory.* [Brokenness]

Nate. *At the time, we met, I attempted to rephrase the question as, 'What is the source of the hope within you?' but I now realize that was my attempt to rationalize hope. However, hope seems to be an irrational quality of mankind that is arguably our greatest strength; without it, we're nothing more than machines. In essence, capacity for hope is what makes us human. I often feel hope with no rational source or reason. Why? I don't know. A higher power? A soul?* [Physics + Astrology]

Rabur. *Thanks for capturing my story. I was shocked by the title of the chapter (Principled Living); you nailed it! You captured the story beautifully; I don't have anything to add or delete.* [Principled Living]

Sharon. *As I read the life stories, I felt thoughtful, encouraged, and sometimes saddened and reflective. You told my story well, and I am pleased with your accounting. Thank you for sharing my story.* [Unresolved]

Thom. *Your interpersonal gift to probe tactfully is best in class and would make Charlie Rose jealous.* [Peace]

Todd. *The draft of The Query came at a very difficult time, but it was at the right moment. Reading this gave me a boost when I needed it. Since we met, we have continued to be blessed. We also have been subjected to many trials but perhaps those are for another chapter. Despite all of them, we still would respond to your query in the same fashion and with an even greater hope.* [Everything Changed]

From Industry

Linda Bobbitt. The Query *follows Larry as he seeks to understand hope by asking perfect strangers to answer a question: 'What is the reason for the hope that is within you?' Their answers, as varied as their backgrounds, are surprising, heart-breaking, and inspirational. As each story unfolds, so does Larry. What began as a somewhat reluctant and clumsy response to an insistent nudge from God becomes a grace-filled habit that has inspired me to explore my own reason for hope.* [Vice President, GeoSpatial Experts, Inc.]

Bray Brunkhurst. *In life, we sometimes need to stop moving, be still, and just listen to the hearts of others. In* The Query, *the author presents the reader with a unique opportunity to simply listen to the uninterrupted and personal stories as fellow travelers unexpectedly share 'the reason for the hope that is within them'. The various vignettes provide a vibrant tapestry of religious and non-religious responses that will touch, inspire, and challenge you.* [Principal, Per4mance Development and Consulting]

Mike Clark. *The stories of real lives working through their challenges, pain, anguish, fear, and ultimately hope have touched me deeply. They have provided inspiration to reach further as I grasp for God's presence (the Holy Spirit) to be the guiding light in my life and my family. To be the reason for my hope. I doubt these stories could be read in one sitting, or even in a short period of time, as each conjures thoughts of how the Spirit works in all people's lives: sometimes subtly, sometimes with a jolt, and sometimes with a sudden conviction. They are jewels of the finest kind.* [Plant Manager, Berry Plastics]

Gerard Ferguson. *... a very interesting and inspirational collection of stories about the challenges many people encounter in their faith journey. It provides valuable perspective for all of us as the author helps each person identify and articulate the reason for hope within them. Anyone who reads this book and contemplates its theme will find a parallel in their own life and a deeper understanding of the reason for hope within them.* [Senior Vice President, EbroNA]

Burnie Lenau. *... great and inspiring, makes you believe the world is going to be alright during these tumultuous times.* [President and CEO, Lawnman, Inc.]

Karsten Lundring. *Fascinating! An easy style to read. In so many of the stories, there is intertwined the history of personal struggle with religion/spirituality/church. Part of my personal hope was diminished as I saw this as a repeating theme. It has made me look at my own national church and wonder whether, in a generation or two, it will still be a means of life support and hope as it has been for our family.* [Co-Managing Partner, Southwest Region, Thrivent Financial]

George Lytal. *An inspirational work. All stories had an effect on me. The fact that no one denied sharing their story is noteworthy and, in itself, merits further exploring. I truly feel that without hope, we die.* [President & CEO, Crestwood Behavioral Health, Inc.]

Wes Oestreich. *Most of us don't take time to pause and reflect about faith and its effect in our lives. Maybe routine itself becomes an enemy of hope. Through the progression of the stories, it is very clear that the author's process and query become more sophisticated over time. His personal quest becomes wrapped up in theirs, so that The Query itself becomes a very interesting journey. It serves as a non-scientific study of the human faith condition ... a snapshot into personal lives that we don't normally share.* [President, Cheever Construction Company]

Les Robins. *The gripping details of private conversations with complete strangers are utterly amazing. The stories are heartwarming and real. Just normal people, telling about their lives, recorded in a way that keeps you yearning for more.* [CPA and small business entrepreneur]

Lisa Smith. *I am struck by the courage and kindness of the author as he genuinely listens to the heartfelt stories of strangers. The Query has caused me to think about our culture, materialism, lack of connectedness with each other and perhaps too much shallow web-connectedness. Which leads me to my take-away: '... and do so with gentleness and respect ...' may have less to do with how the content is received, than how necessary it is that the content be delivered. Delivering one's message of hope gently and respectfully opens one's heart to feel, contemplate and perhaps understand oneself better; to release, to reminisce, to feel.* [President, Effective HR Solutions, LLC]

Jeff Tritapoe. *... I found my emotions and thoughts aligned with each story; I could sympathize or empathize with each one. My progression through the book was therapeutic, and I would recommend The Query to anyone contemplating their position in life.* [Vice President of Quality and Process Engineering, Xerium Technologies, Inc.]

Howard Vreeland. *I could not stop reading once I started. The Query is moving, thought provoking, uplifting.* [President & CEO, Anderson & Vreeland, Inc.]

Vic Williams. *… the whole idea of approaching total strangers in 'intimate' settings and posing them all the same question takes guts. Surprises arise and enlightenment happens. Most people don't think they have a story to tell, but The Query proves otherwise.* [Executive Editor, Madavor Media LLC]

From Church Professionals

The Rev. Lonnie Bullock. *The Query is both inspiring and challenging. I was inspired by the honesty and transparency of people as they talked about the reason for their hope. I was challenged to review and be able to articulate the reason for my hope. The author models a great example of how to have spiritual conversations in a natural and non-threatening way by simply talking about the reason for hope. For those wanting to be inspired and be better prepared to have spiritual conversation, The Query is a great read.* [Executive Director, New Church Specialties]

The Rev. Bill Easum. *The writing is excellent. It's not easy to write conversations. I was intrigued with the stories. It's good stuff!* [Founder and Principal, 21st Century Strategies, Inc., and author of numerous books on church dynamics (including his personal favorite, *Turning Dreams into Reality*)]

The Rev. Kathryn Gulbranson. *Taken as a whole, the stories speak to the truth that people want and need to process their life, to make sense of their life and, in most cases, their relationship with God. These stories also say so much about hope, which is at the core of our lives of faith. On a personal level, The Query has encouraged me to consider the hope which is within me. It has inspired me to consider all that I have to be grateful for and to give thanks to God for it.* [Co-Pastor, Marin Lutheran Church]

The Rev. Dr. Richard Johnson. *I found The Query very interesting – more so than I really expected. The stories are captivating and intriguing, every one of them.* [Affiliate Associate Professor of Church History, Fuller Theological Seminary]

The Rev. Brian Malison. *In* The Query, *we are given the privilege of eavesdropping on intimate, holy conversations. To have people share their deep dark secrets, or at least the things that evoke an emotional response, is so powerful. That alone is worth more than anything in this collection.*

This book has led me to appreciate the value of the 1 Peter verse, and the importance for each of us to answer. I have read that passage literally a hundred times but have never been gripped by it, until now. So, what is my answer? How do I define "hope" in my life? I don't think I'm nearly as prepared to give an answer as I think I am. But how deeply important to understand hope, to define it in oneself, and to embrace it.

The underlying reality of these encounters is that the author has been led by a spirit other than his own. And that alone is worth greater reflection. How do we hear the promptings of the Holy Spirit in relation to conversations we need to have with others – strangers or not? I have been profoundly moved in reading this significant project. [Senior Pastor, Christ Lutheran Church]

The Rev. Dr. Clay Schmit. *Every person's life is a drama, made up of countless episodes or stories. Larry Moeller has decided to be intentional about stories which have enriched his life. And, delightfully, he has decided to share them with us. This collection of intentional episodes is engaging and inspiring. Chance encounters have become parables brought to us by the discerning poetry of* The Query. *Reading this book will help you to see the light of Christ in the people that you encounter in the episodes of your own life.* [Provost, Lutheran Theological Southern Seminary – Lenoir-Rhyne University]

The Rev. Thomas Skrenes. *Larry Moeller has done here what so many of us think needs to be done: find out why people have 'hope'. The human condition is eternally fascinating and in these brief interviews, Larry gets to it. "Why do we live?", and "How shall we live?" In listening to the stories of others, we learn what makes for a meaningful life for ourselves.* [Bishop, Northern Great Lakes Synod, Evangelical Lutheran Church in America]

The Rev. Christine Slaughter. *It was a great joy to read. The question about hope in our lives causes one to think deeply. The 'one on one' approach is awesome, which leads me to believe that The Query would be an excellent model for evangelizing. This verse from scripture makes it easy to enter into a conversation with a stranger, who may not know the Lord. And it leads the Christian to share their source of hope. Plus, the stories reflect a good cross-section of individuals.* [Pastor, Robinson Chapel AME Church]

The Rev. Dr. Phil Stevenson. *The first I heard of The Query, I was hooked. You will be compelled by what the author has learned. You will be drawn in by the stories he shares. You will be challenged to more fully grasp the hope you have. And, you may even find God tapping on your shoulder.* [Assistant District Superintendent, Pacific-Southwest District, Wesleyan Church]

The Rev. Brian Stein-Webber. *Larry Moeller takes us on an ever-deepening exploration into how much we want to share our stories with one another, even with a total stranger. He shows that a kind word and a listening ear are all it takes to uncover 'the reason for the hope that is within us.' The fact that only a minority of responses have specific theological content should also indicate to us how the world has changed, and how we might change our own evangelism efforts.* [Director of Seminary Relations, Pacific Lutheran Theological Seminary}

The Rev. Tim Wright. *Each story captivates. The author has an amazing gift to allow God's spirit to enter into a conversation and make it holy and sacred. The insights into life as people live it (especially those without a faith foundation) are so very important for us Christians to hear. Many of the stories affirm what Luther says ... that God meets us in the despair of life. That's where God is most visible.* [Pastor, Community of Grace, and author of numerous books including his most recent work, *Searching for Tom Sawyer: How Parents and Congregations Can Stop the Exodus of Boys from Church. www.TimWrightMinistries.org*]

Dedicated to –

Helen, the bravest person I know . . .

and

Les, the most steadfast.

A Note from the Author

The Query is a collection of stories - stories of hope - arising from a simple question: "What is the reason for the hope that is within you?"

They were gathered through chance encounters with strangers across America: On airplanes, in restaurants or cafés, at a car dealership, in a jury waiting room. The stories are as diverse as the storytellers: a teen anticipating senior prom in the arms of her first love; a crusty construction superintendent; an engaging nuclear physicist; a widow scarred by life, with no hope; a Catholic priest on assignment in Rome; a long-haul truck driver; an Army colonel with tours in Bosnia, Iraq, and Afghanistan; a seasoned executive in the twilight of career; a thrice-married divorcee yearning for another chance; an eager young Polish immigrant, now a Fortune 500 engineer; and many more.

Readers eavesdrop on deeply personal conversations as stories unfold. They are struck by a sad truth when Todd, the bankruptcy attorney and attentive husband in the story 'Everything Changed', shares: *"I've been reflecting that we don't really take the time to listen to people anymore."*

Often the stories turn to matters of faith. Some story tellers found hope through church in the middle of despair. For others, church or religion was a source of hurt, leading the author to observe:

> "I wonder. How would a faith community – a church, a mosque, a synagogue, a temple – be perceived differently if it became known above all as *the people who listen*, and not *the people who preach*?"

The Epilogue invites and challenges the reader to gather stories of hope, with a step-by-step guide for doing so. In becoming *people who listen* rather than *people who preach*, the author foresees a sweeping cultural course correction in America, grounded in a simple query of hope.

The Query is also a journey. Interwoven with the stories is the journey of one man's struggle to overcome fear arising from a simple text:

Always be prepared to answer the question when someone asks of the reason for the hope that is within you, and do so with gentleness and respect.

The fear? How to answer the question were someone to ask. The struggle is compared to that of learning to ride a bicycle. It began in uncertainty, and became a journey of joy.

Privacy considerations meant changing some identifying details including names and geographies, with the exception of these names: Bruce and Mike, Pastor Al, Mary, Bill and Lee, and Pastor Ron. They are real.

So are the stories.

Larry Moeller

The Query

I.	*A Deep Compelling*	15
	Journal Entry	17
	The Leader	21
	Insights: *A Deep Compelling*	29
II.	*The Novice*	33
	Peace	35
	Clarity	39
	Empty	45
	Purpose	48
	Secrets	51
	Rethinking	57
	Insights: *The Novice*	62
III.	*Brief Encounters*	65
	Separation	67
	Parental Pride	71
	Larger Purpose	73
	Jury Duty	75
	Potential	78
	Insights: *Brief Encounters*	82
IV.	*Listening*	83
	Invasive Love	85
	Two-by-Four	92
	Favorites	101
	Unresolved	106
	Principled Living	110
	Everything Changed	117
	Balance	123
	Physics + Astrology	130
	Broken Trust	135
	Insights: *Listening*	142

V. *Engaged*	147
Always 'Always'	149
Critical Analysis	158
Shattered Dream	171
A Common Basis	185
Brokenness	194
Epilogue I: *Reflections*	206
Epilogue II: *A Movement*	209
Appendix: *Study Resource*	218
Acknowledgements	221
About the Author	223

I. A Deep Compelling

He was three when the bicycle arrived. It was early Christmas morning, and my excitement mirrored Ethan's as he bounded into the living room. His wide eyes quickly surveyed the spread of presents and then popped when he saw it tucked behind the tree. "Grampa, is that bike for me?" he cried.

The morning couldn't fly by fast enough. Presents and candy, and the special Christmas breakfast. But Ethan's imagining was already gliding around the vast expanse of the empty parking lot at the nearby school. "Is it time, Grampa? Can we go now?"

Soon we were on the porch, bundled for the winter chill with the last task remaining. But not for Ethan. "No, Grampa, I don't need those," he sneered at the training wheels. "They're for little kids."

Trembling with excitement, he straddled the gleaming fire-engine red bicycle. Suddenly, the fear of uncertainty set in.

"You'll be okay, Ethan," I said. "Trust the one whose hand is on your shoulder."

A Deep Compelling describes the unexpected launch of *The Query* through a life-changing experience.

Journal Entry	17
The Leader	21
Insights: ***A Deep Compelling***	29

Journal Entry

It was a somber flight. Ninety minutes, early morning. Fairbanks to Anchorage.

I've had two relationships in my adult life. The first, a marriage of 32 years. The second, just concluded. It had been a delight-filled relationship after several years of close friendship. Our decision to 'dial back' the relationship from romance and intimacy to deep friendship was the right decision.

So, the flight was the beginning of the next chapter of life, stepping back into loneliness on the way to 'alone-ness'. Aloneness isn't so bad. In the time after the marriage ended, I had learned that passing through loneliness to aloneness was painful. So, the flight was bound to begin on a somber note and the unfolding journal entries reflected that. Through the years, journaling has been my rear-view mirror. The growing collection of journals serve as a mirror into my past through which later understanding often comes.

Just outside the window, so close as to touch it, the spectacle of snow-covered Mt. McKinley – Denali awash from brilliant sun – caught me short. In a time of darkness of soul, a dazzling light. Amazing.

Journal entry:

> *July 7, 2009. Tuesday morn ... enroute, Fairbanks to Anchorage ... departure from AK. Will I ever return? Probably not. Probably not. And so, we part, Linda and I. Forever? God only knows. God only knows. Linda's deep fear: So alone except for you, Lord Jesus. Her plea to me, "Pray for my soul."*

I put down the pen, and prayed for her soul. It was a somber flight. Ahead, the Anchorage-Seattle leg.

Journal entry:

> *July 7, 2009 (cont.). Time for reflections ... this Flight 84, Alaska Air ... Anchorage to Seattle ... 3+ hours.*

Here I am, at age 60 ... my life two-thirds through ... entering the final third. What have been meaningful accomplishments? Family: children, a grandson. Faith journey: a testimony to God's presence in my life. Professional: twenty years in the corporate world, followed by eighteen in executive search. In all, lives enhanced.

More important than past accomplishments, what shall be the nature of the next thirty years? What shall be at their core? To give and receive love. To grow ever deeper in faith. Indeed, the interweaving of faith with the giving and receiving of love.

Through the last twenty years, my vocation ... my life calling ... has been to devote time and resource to these purposes. In recent years, I have been pulled by matters of 'church', and of personal relationship. These have guided my life activities.

Lord Jesus, I seem to be entering a time of fallow. Purpose is still ever present, but the vision for living it out has yet to unfold. The reality of endings and beginnings in our lives. "We are Easter people ... the old must die, for new life to come" (Pastor Al).

Letting the past be the past. The past belongs to the past. Leave it there. Embrace what is to come.

'If the vision tarries ... wait.' Habakkuk.

This is enough for now. Enough of a vision: giving and receiving love; letting go of the old, while awaiting and embracing the new. Living into a time of emptiness, and awaiting the new.

Setting the journal aside with window seat reclined, thoughts swirled of the weekend past and the unknown of what may come. An hour or so had passed in the pleasure of unhurried journaling. Time had seemed to stop.

The quiet pondering was suddenly interrupted by an unlikely intruder: a disturbing Bible verse from my past. Several years earlier during a morning devotion, a text from 1 Peter had unsettled me: *Always be prepared to give the answer to the question when someone asks of the reason for the hope that is within you ... and do so with gentleness and respect.*

At the time, I shared 1 Peter 3:15 with my weekly breakfast buddies, Bruce and Mike – and my fear that if someone *were* to ask, I wasn't sure how to answer. "Forget it," they counseled, "no one will ever ask. So, stop fretting." With a nervous laugh, the fear was dismissed.

So why this text, now? It had left me for months. Why was it returning now, of all times, given the recent parting? I pushed it aside.

Journaling continued, following other thoughts. But the verse would not leave, and the discomfort returned. Once again I found myself wrestling with feelings of inadequacy over how to answer the question were someone to ask.

Many have experienced and written of the 'still, small voice' of God. It may come through a sunset or snow covered peaks, in spring flowers or crackling thunderstorms, a baby's cry or a child's laugh, through the antics of lambs or the song of a meadowlark. We are often encouraged to be attentive to the 'still, small voice' of God.

But on this flight, in this window seat, at this moment the voice of God was neither still nor small. In those rare moments when God has spoken clearly to me, it has not been through idle pleasantries or glimpses of paradise; rather, it has been so foreign and brings such extreme discomfort that it marks the certainty of a life shift ahead. It has happened twice before.

During journaling and once again wrestling with the discomfort of 1 Peter, an intense clarity gripped me:

> *"Larry, quit worrying about how you are going to answer the question. I want you to ask it."*

The pen fell from my fingers, and I looked around. Nothing. No grand movement. No spectacle. The plane and its passengers were quiet, everyone settled peacefully into the long flight.

No problem, as the thought raced through my mind. I'll ask the question … sometime.

> *"No, not sometime. Today. On this flight. Now."*

The open journal was staring back at me. What in the world was this about? Before me, a critical moment. A moment to decide whether to act as so clearly compelled, or to push it aside. I reflected on the two times when the compelling was so strong that it could not be ignored: one, about fifteen years earlier; the second, a couple years ago. Each time, my life took an abrupt turn. The compelling this time was equally powerful, equally discomforting. But now? And how, for heaven's sake? How?

The next chapter of my life was about to unfold. Little did I know the thrill God had in mind as the page turned.

The Leader

*"Faith, it is said, is better than belief,
because belief is when someone else does the thinking."*
Mitch Albom, from *The First Phone Call from Heaven*[1]

The window seat near the rear meant boarding in an early group. So, watching the baggage handlers scurry about on the Anchorage tarmac helped fill the time as passengers slowly made their way down the aisle. Perhaps luck would bring an empty middle seat. It's nice to have elbow room on long flights, and the several hours of un-cramped solitude would be very welcome.

The plea of the airline attendant for volunteers to take later flights because of overbooking took care of that. The flight would be full. Who would be sharing this space?

He was wearing a cap, had a visible limp, and a cane in his right hand. He looked to be a little older than I, a little taller, with a bit of a hunch. Glasses. T-shirt and jeans.

After stowing the cane above, he slowly lowered himself into the middle seat and smiled. There were gaps in the smile. Here we were, two tall men scrunched side by side in another of today's modern airliners. It would be a cozy four hours by the time we got to the gate in Seattle.

He had no reading material, which seemed odd for a long flight. He was motionless, stoic, arms on his lap and hands on his knees, cap atop his head, eyes forward. By occasional glances, I noticed muscular arms with big hands. They were worker hands, though clean – no stains in the creases. As we gained cruising altitude, he sat very still … erect … staring straight ahead, while I focused on articles from the latest issue of *The Economist*, then the Anchorage newspaper, and finally the crossword. The silence was welcome.

We'd been in the air for at least an hour, and my seatmate hadn't stirred. Upright, eyes forward, hands on knees, silent.

He seemed oblivious to all around him, and most assuredly to the 1 Peter discomfort which had me so firmly in its grip:

"I want you to ask the question. Today. On this flight. Now."

How in heaven's name do I do this, now? *"Uh, excuse me, but, uh, what is the reason for the hope that is within you?"* This was crazy!!!

Yet, the compelling was unfading. So, best to sneak up on it.

I turned toward him. "Going home, or going visiting?"

His head turned, but nothing else moved. He looked at me, and replied politely, "Going visiting."

Oh. Where to?

"Idaho ... to Twin Falls."

What takes you there?

"My in-laws. They're getting up there in years, and their home needs a little tending, so I'm going to spend a few weeks doing some fix-up stuff."

Odd. He walked with a limp and relied on a cane, and he's going to do remodeling!

So, a honey-do list for the in-laws?

"Yes," he chuckled. "They're good folks."

Where's home?

"Ketchikan."

How long have you lived there?

"Oh, about thirty years."

Kids? Grandkids?

"Yeah," he smiled. "Married three times. Three kids with Wife No. 1 ... 10 years, and three kids. Then Wife No. 2 ... three-four years. After marriage No. 2, I was pretty much convinced I would never meet or need another woman.

"Then, I met a woman at a community food closet through my church. I grilled her ... gave her the 'Ten Questions'. She was surprised to ever hear from me again. I put her through quite a grilling. But now she's Wife No. 3. We've been married 8 years, and we're happy. Got six grandkids scattered around ... mine and hers."

"Wow!" I exclaimed. "I just turned 60, and I only have *one* grandchild! How lucky for you. You must have started young!"

"Yep," he admitted, "I guess we started too young. Maybe that was part of the problem in my first marriage. And, I turned 60 a couple months ago, myself."

I pondered a bit, reflecting. Wondering how to continue. Then, "So, 60. Vietnam?"

"Yep," he replied.

Did you serve there?

"Yeah. I was a heavy equipment operator. Best duty an 18-year-old could get. Ten months running a Caterpillar tractor all day, clearing away jungle for landing strips. I loved it!"

And after Vietnam?

"Got married and moved to Ketchikan. Became a carpet layer, for 30 years. Got a boat. Enjoy fishing and being outdoors."

Retired?

"No. I teach folks about energy conservation in their homes and help them make upgrades so they save money on heating bills. Heating bills can get pretty steep in Alaska, and for older folks on fixed incomes, it can be tough."

That's great ... and quite a change from carpet laying. How did you get into that?

He turned quiet for a moment, tears welling up. "Well, two years ago, there was a heavy snow. I was clearing my driveway when someone came barreling down the street and lost control. The car slammed into me ... broke my neck, leg, ankle, severe internal injuries, lost some teeth. Five months in bed. Wife No. 3 tended me day and night. She's quite a woman, and I'm lucky to have her in my life."

We were both quiet for a bit.

I extended my hand. "Hi. My name is Larry. I've gotta know who I'm talking with."

"I'm Quentin," he smiled. "Nice to meet you."

We sat for a few more minutes. I pondered how to proceed. Then ...

"You've had quite some life experiences," I started. "Vietnam. Two broken marriages. Kids and grandkids scattered around. A terrible accident that changed everything."

"Yes," he reflected softly. "I've been through a lot."

"Quentin, I'm going to ask a question and if it's uncomfortable or inappropriate, just say so. Given what's happened in your life, I wonder. Are you a religious man?"

"Yes," he said. "I'm a Christian."

"I know this could get kind of personal, but I wonder what part faith has played in your life journey? Can you share?"

Quentin turned silent and resumed his eyes-forward pose. After a moment, he shifted and looked intently into my eyes. The conversation turned intimate.

"I was raised Roman Catholic," he began. "My mom, bless her heart, was a devout Catholic until the day she died.

"When I got to Vietnam, someone gave me a Bible. I spent a lot of time in it. It was in the Bible that I came to know God. I never knew God in the church I was raised in. It was big on ritual. Whatever the priest told us, that was what we were supposed to believe. How could I come to know the Bible when I was relying on the priest to read and interpret it? My understanding was his understanding. It was only after I began to spend time in the Bible that God became meaningful to me. Until the Army, the Bible just wasn't a part of my life.

"But that changed in Vietnam. So, when I got out, I looked for a church where the Bible was important to it. Through the years, I've belonged to several Bible churches. Eight years ago, while at the food ministry in my church, I met the woman who would become my wife. We've been there ever since. My faith is an important part of my life."

"Thank you for sharing, Quentin. That is really encouraging." I paused, trying to figure out how to continue.

"Do you know who Peter is, in the Bible?"

"Sure," he chuckled, a twinkle in his eye. "Is this a test?"

We laughed. I shared a little of my faith journey ... of the impact of occasional bible verses ... and in recent years, I Peter 3:15: *"Always be prepared to give the answer to the question when somebody asks of the reason for the hope that is within you. And do so with gentleness and respect ... "*.

We reflected on Peter, and wondered whether Peter, bold and brash Peter, would suggest 'gentleness and respect'. When I shared that I felt off the hook because it seems unlikely anyone will ever put the question to me in those precise words, he chuckled again.

For a few minutes, we sat silently. Then, I turned to Quentin.

"Quentin," I began, "I'm going to risk one more question. I can't shake that verse. And it came to me earlier today that God wants me to be *asking* the question. I don't know why, but that's what I'm supposed to do. So, I'm going to ask you. *What is the reason for the hope that is within you?"*

He turned and studied me. His eyes moistened. Silently he turned to face forward. Then softly, "That would be Jesus Christ."

We sat for a few moments. I was unsure where to go from there.

"You know, Quentin," I admitted, "I've never done this before, but I have a feeling I'm going to be doing it a lot more. And I don't know whether I'll ever hear a better answer – but I'm not sure I know what you mean. So, can we go a little deeper? What does that mean, that 'Jesus Christ' is the reason for your hope? What do you mean by that?"

Again, Quentin looked into my eyes while his moistened even more.

"For all my adult life," he began, "from as far back as I can remember, I saw myself as invincible. There was nothing I couldn't do … nowhere I couldn't go … nothing I couldn't say. I was the invincible man.

"Two years ago, in an instant, that changed. For five months, flat on my back, I learned what it was like to be fully dependent on someone else. I learned what it was like to have someone beside me morning and night. To take care of me because I could not.

"I came to know Jesus in those five months. He brought me through to where I am today.

"Jesus is my leader." Then, he fell silent.

I reflected on his answer, and probed further. "What do you mean … your leader?"

"Were you in the military?" he asked.

No.

"You would need to have been in the military to really understand that. He's always in front. He gave himself up completely. That's what a leader does. He died on the cross for my sin. I believe that. He is the reason for the hope inside me. It's Jesus."

We sat again in silence. A powerful silence.

"Quentin," I said, "I don't know what's ahead with this. But there's a reason God sat us next to each other. And it seems that whether next week, or next year, or 5 years from now, I may want to get back in touch with you. Would you be willing to share your home address so I can?"

He did.

For quite a while, we enjoyed meaningful conversation around family and faith. He shared how he learned to do door-to-door evangelism by posing three questions: 1) Do you believe that when you die, you will go to heaven? 2) Why, or why not? 3) Would you like to learn more? We talked of ways of personal witness in a culture where faith conversations seldom happen beyond the walls of a church.

"Do you have a favorite Bible verse, or one which has spoken to you the most these last few years?" I asked.

"No one verse," he replied. "I don't like it when people, preachers, pull out phrases and twist them to their way of thinking. I need to see all of it, not just the pieces.

"What about you? Do you have a favorite verse, other than 1 Peter 3:15?" he laughed.

We talked about 2 Timothy 1:6: *"...fan into flame the gift of God that is within you ... for you have been given a spirit not of timidity but of power, and of love, and of self-control."*

And from Oswald Chambers, *My Utmost for His Highest*[2], his January 31 devotion which begins: *"Our primary calling is not to be holy men and women, but to be proclaimers of the gospel of God."*

Too soon, the announcement came of the approach to Sea-Tac. As he rose to retrieve his cane, he bid safe travel; we grasped hands with a firmness that only intimate familiarity brings.

Once in the terminal, I scurried to an airline shop, bought a Moleskine© notebook[3], and settled into Starbucks for the two-hour layover to Sacramento – and wrote, capturing the experience and conversation before it would fade.

And so was launched ... *The Query*.

A story shared ... a blessing received.

Footnotes:

[1] *The First Phone Call from Heaven*, by Mitch Albom. Copyright © 2013 by ASOP, Inc. Harper Collins Publishers, 10 East 53rd Street, New York, NY 10022. (ISBN: 978-0-06-229437-1)

[2] Taken from *My Utmost for His Highest* by Oswald Chambers, © 1935 by Dodd Mead & Co., renewed © 1963 by Oswald Chambers Publications Assn., Ltd., and is used by permission of Discovery House Publishers, Box 3566, Grand Rapids, Michigan 49501. All rights reserved.

[3] Moleskine© is a trademark of Syntegra Capital with US offices at Moleskine® America, Inc., 210 Eleventh Avenue, Suite 1004, New York NY 10001. Telephone (646) 461-3018. www.moleskine.com

Insights: *A Deep Compelling*

Extreme discomfort.

Trust.

Surrender.

The three dimensions of living into a *Deep Compelling*: Extreme discomfort. Trust. Surrender.

It is easy to compartmentalize faith within the routine of life. Confining it to a Sunday morning box keeps the 'God mystery' tolerable. And comfortable. When the 'God mystery' stays within the box, life ambles along peacefully. To be sure, midweek prayer life and devotionals offer a touch of inspiration. But the Sunday morning box is where the 'God mystery' lives, and where it belongs.

But then there comes a *Deep Compelling*. The 'God mystery' takes a stroll, interrupts the routine, and resets the course. Sometimes the *Deep Compelling* comes in a dramatic life event. Or in a momentary revealing out of the blue. Or through a long process of step-by-step learning until clarity surprises. Or, perhaps the *Deep Compelling* comes through a chance encounter with a book. However, and whenever, the 'God mystery' chuckles when the awakening comes.

In the birth experience of *The Query*, my discomfort with I Peter 3:15 had been eclipsed by a far greater discomfort because of this *Deep Compelling*. It wasn't simply the instructive to "quit worrying about how you are going to answer the question. I want you to ask it." No, that wouldn't be so difficult. That's an assignment for the Sunday morning box when surrounded by like-minded sojourners who also seek understanding of the 'God mystery'. Actually, the instructive relieved me of the personal discomfort with the verse. I could pose the question with people and in places of my choosing, on my terms. No problem.

"No, not sometime. Today. On this flight. Now."

And at that moment, the extreme discomfort. The 'God mystery' had left its Sunday morning box, stepped onto an airliner over the skies of Alaska, and engaged as the Great Discomforter. This wasn't the Wonderful Counselor, the Mighty God, the Everlasting Father, the Prince of Peace. [1] No. Yet again, the 'God mystery' had intruded in my life as the Great Discomforter.

Have you experienced the Great Discomforter? No? Well, you will. The beauty and the joy of the intrusion is in its surprise.

You have? Then you have also experienced the next dimension of the *Deep Compelling*. Trust. Is this *Deep Compelling* before me a fleeting thought, a momentary emotion? Or is it something more, something greater, of a source or substance beyond imagining? Most important, is this compelling to be trusted?

"Today. On this flight. Now."

This was not of my imagining. How could I possibly imagine such a directive? Part of the proof lay in the gnawing persistence of the 1 Peter verse through the years. It was time to confront it, but in a way I could not have imagined. Yes, this compelling could be trusted.

So next, the most critical dimension of a *Deep Compelling*. Surrender.

My roots grew deep on an Iowa farm. Early morning barnyard chores had to be finished before breakfast and before the school bus arrived. Same, but in reverse at the end of the day. That discipline, plus swinging a hammer in Dad's contracting business during college breaks, shaped my respect for work. Little did I know that it would pay dividends during the early years of career, eventually leading to general manager of a division of a Fortune 500 firm. And later, as the co-founder and owner of a small business which endured the most severe economic meltdown since the Great Depression. Work hard. Be diligent. Map the strategy. Work the plan.

Surrendering to the *Deep Compelling* flies in the face of who and what I am. It is, for me, the most difficult. Experiencing an extreme discomfort, okay. Trusting it, I can get there. But acting on it ... surrendering to it ... letting it disrupt my living. Therein lies the proverbial 'where the rubber meets the road.'

"Ok, God. I'm gonna do it. I will ask the question. Today. On this flight. But please, God. Please help me. And don't leave me hanging … please don't leave me hanging. Amen." A simple, earnest prayer.

And along comes Quentin. Outwardly, he would be someone with whom I normally would be unlikely to engage. But while wrestling with how to proceed, recalling Jesus' encouragement to the Twelve helped:

> *"…do not worry about what to say or how to say it. At that time, you will be given what to say, for it will not be you speaking, but the Spirit of your Father speaking through you."* [2]

The encounter with Quentin was the beginning of a life shift. Certainly, for me. And probably, in some way, for Quentin. God only knows.

The stories and insights comprising *The Query* are a part of that life shift. What more does God have in mind with *The Query*? God knows. Maybe the stories in *The Query* will offer some insight into the presence of the 'God mystery'. Or maybe *The Query* is the time of your deep compelling.

The words of encouragement to Ethan on that first wobbly bike ride were just as fitting for the wobbly start of *The Query*:

Trust the One whose hand is on your shoulder.

Footnotes:

[1] Isaiah 9:6

[2] Matthew 10:19-20

II. The Novice

The ride was slow and jerky, filled with stops and starts. Grampa's grasp on his shoulder was at times firm, at times gentle, but always present. We were back on the porch, after what for Ethan had been a frustrating first bicycle ride. There was going to be more to learning to ride a bike than he had imagined.

"Ok, Grampa," he was convinced. "I guess I need the training wheels. At least until I get good."

On came the training wheels. The second ride was better than the first, and the third ride better than the second. It takes a while to learn the basics.

It's all about balance.

- - - - - - - - - - - - - - - -

The Novice presents the initial encounters of this businessman-turned-listener. As with a beginning bicyclist, practice improves outcome. The stories are shorter and reflect the uncertainty of a novice story gatherer.

Peace	35
Clarity	39
Empty	45
Purpose	48
Secrets	51
Rethinking	57
Insights: *The Novice*	62

Peace

"The Lord lift up his countenance upon you and give you peace."
Numbers 6:26 (NRSV)

He was the kind of guy who puts people instantly at ease: energetic, with an engaging smile. The baseball cap, tee shirt, shorts, and running shoes testified to his enthusiasm.

"Great morning, isn't it!" he exclaimed as he settled into the middle seat and extended his hand. "I'm Thom. What's your name? I always want to know who I'm sitting beside." His smile broadened even more.

"I'm Larry," I chuckled. "Did they put an extra espresso in your Starbucks this morning?" He laughed.

We enjoyed the banter of the Southwest attendant as he put us through the paces of preparing for the flight to Nashville from San Diego. His contrast of the balminess we were leaving, to the sultriness of July in Tennessee, had everyone atwitter. It was another instance of the good-natured whimsy which has endeared the culture of Southwest Airlines to the flying public.

Conversation flowed easily and family stories began to unfold. Thom is one of three children, all with Scandinavian first names. His mom was a teacher. "Dad was a dreamer. I get my drive from my mom," he smiled.

He has two young sons, age 4 and 2, and a daughter on the way. His wife is the homemaker and stay-at-home mom "because family is important to us." After earning his degree, he signed up as part of the sales team with a telecommunications company and has been with them for 15 years. As a national account manager, he enjoys his work. "They've treated me well. It's a great company."

It's easy to see why Thom has done well. He is very engaging with a knack for probing without being intrusive. He was curious about life lessons and what he could learn from mine. Since my two sons and daughter are now adults leading lives of their own, he probed how to raise kids, and the challenges young parents may expect. He was curious around the circumstances which led to my divorce after a long marriage. His sincerity moved me.

Soon, the conversation turned to *The Query*, its basis from 1 Peter, and the recent story of Quentin. He was fascinated.

"The Christian faith is a very important piece of my living," he shared.

Thom was raised Methodist and is now a member of a Brethren church near his home. It (and he) embraces the Bible as a guide to correct living. In that vein, as part of their wedding ceremony, readings from Deuteronomy and Ephesians were included on the roles of husband (as Christ is the husband of the church) and wife (supportive of the husband).

Currently he is studying Ecclesiastes and teaching it to his sons.

"Our church is a grace-based church, not works based," he noted.

"So, Thom, the query," I paused. "*What is the reason for the hope that is within you?*"

He was silent, thoughtful. "A growing understanding of God," he replied, "with God in my life."

How has that given you *'the reason for hope?'*

"I guess it's that Jesus has already taken my sin on Himself. That with all my mistakes, He has forgiven me. That lets me live in peace, and in that is hope."

A story shared ... a blessing received.

[Author's note: Months after mailing the draft of his story to Thom, this pleasant surprise arrived in my inbox. Blessings, indeed!]

Subject: 'Peace' … *The Query*
From: "Thom"
Date: Tue 5/6/2014 9:21 am
To: querier@risenindeed.com

Larry,

'Thom' checking in. So, sorry for the silence. Life with three kids, work, church, and coaching kids makes extra anything a bit of a commitment. However, I've just finished *Rethinking* and enjoyed the calling card you have to capture the reason for the hope that is within us. The stories reveal the brokenness in this world and the power of our risen Lord indeed.

I was in an extra good mood on the day of our flight probably because I had been on an overbooked Southwest flight that day and received a check for full fare. I was going to Nashville unexpectedly for a God-ordained moment with you.

Just one more quick note today. I have recently joined our local church as an elder and during that process I was asked about divorce and remarriage, and after your discussion in the story *Brokenness*, I thought it was worthwhile sharing a hard-to-find book on divorce and remarriage by Mykel Pamperin called *Let No Man Put Asunder*. This book seems to address the same topics that you discussed with the Catholic priest. I am in the unique position of learning of my father's two prior marriages before mother later in life. I also know that God's grace covers any sin, so I never dwell in the past … its part of the hope that is within me.

In our discussion, it seems you may be still struggling with the past… normal… but let me tell you, that I think God is using it and you for good now.

I'm sorry to dump and run. I just wanted you to know that I appreciate your work and calling to shed light on God's marvelous creation of the human race. Your interpersonal gift to probe tactfully is best in class and would make Charlie Rose jealous.

I'll be back in touch and be praying for you and your project.

Blessings.

"Thom"

Clarity

*"If the vision tarries, wait for it;
it will surely come ... "*
a paraphrase, Habakkuk 2:3

He was the last of the C group on another full Southwest Airlines flight, bound for San Jose from Nashville. While many fliers like the efficiency of Southwest and its approach to seating, from the look on his face as he came down the aisle, he didn't seem to be one of them. When you're at the tail end of C, you take what you get. Hal got me.

At first glance, he had the look of an engineer: average height and build, pale, thirtyish, glasses, clean shaven, an earnest demeanor. He settled into the middle seat, craning his neck to follow another late boarder as she passed by. With a smile in her direction, he turned forward and settled in.

A co-worker? "No," he said, "my wife. It's times like these when I wish Southwest had pre-assigned seats. We wanted to sit together, but checked in too late, so the high numbers and now we're a couple of rows apart."

It had been only two weeks since that first life-changing *Query* experience. Already I was finding that when things seemed a little out of the ordinary, curiosity of an underlying story trumped any natural tendency to remain aloof.

He seemed older than the typical newlywed. "How long have you been married?" I asked.

His eyes lit up. "Only 2 years," he beamed. Hal and Yva found each other on e-Harmony.com. He was in California, she in rural Georgia.

"You can probably tell I'm an introvert," he smiled. "It was always hard for me to meet someone and open up. Yva, too. But we're really good for each other and very happy."

Rural Georgia and northern California! That had to be an interesting courtship.

"Oh, yeah," Hal chuckled. "Twelve trips back and forth – and married on Trip 13!"

Life together is new to both of them. With Yva's ticking biological clock and some health problems, it seems children may not be in the cards. "We're just so happy we found each other. People roll their eyes over the e-Harmony thing, but I don't think either of us would be married without it."

As memories around the twelve trips spilled out, his eyes danced. He was clearly enjoying the telling as much as I was enjoying the listening.

We shook hands and shared names. This cross-country flight was going to be anything but run-of-the-mill. As I pulled out *The Query* notebook and shared a little of the experience two weeks before, he was intrigued and willing. Before posing the query, I explained, it would be helpful to learn a little about him.

Hal grew up near Half Moon Bay, a seaside community about forty-five minutes south of San Francisco. With a slight smile and in a wry note, he shared about a 'pain in the neck' that had nothing to do with the person sitting next to him! Scoliosis has been a part of his life for as long as he could remember, with regular exercise and ongoing chiropractic care. The discipline of the water polo team in high school introduced swimming as a part of his regimen. Now he logs several miles a week at the nearby YMCA.

He's 39. As it turned out, Hal *is* an engineer with a California county. For some time, he's been immersed in a project to resurface bridges as part of the ongoing California seismic retrofit program.

Do you enjoy your work?

"It's okay, but sometimes it gets a little boring," he replied. "I've been doing it a while."

As the conversation turned toward faith, Hal's countenance changed. No longer the introvert, he began describing his faith journey.

"Growing up Assemblies of God, speaking in tongues and the presence of the Holy Spirit was routine. As time went by, I drifted from that," he acknowledged. "Yva and I are part of a non-denominational church, and it works for us."

Living the faith is very important to him. Hal shared of his involvement in Engineering Missionaries International since his college days. "It's sort of like 'Doctors without Borders'," he explained. "I was on a five-month mission in northern India a while ago, and more recently an extended trip to Haiti and Honduras. It's a way for me to use my engineering know-how in some pretty dismal places, to help make things better."

The stories about the EMI mission trips filled much of the flight. They were fascinating, and it was clear that he found fulfillment in them.

Three hours had passed quickly.

"Ok, Hal … before this flight gets away from us, here's the query. *What is the reason for the hope that is within you?*"

Even though Hal knew the question was coming, he sat quietly for a few moments with his stare fixed on the seat in front of him. "I've never been asked that before," he said, softly. The silence continued, a comfortable silence. He seemed at peace with the question, simply putting his thoughts in order.

"It's not easy for me to answer that with a simple phrase. It's not something I've thought about. Do I have hope? You bet. But what's the reason for the hope I have?"

More quiet. Then, "Well, there is the expectation of spending eternity with God. And of my own personal need for a savior, and realizing that I am lost without Christ as that savior. These are reasons for my hope.

"But above all, trusting in God's mercy. I am so grateful that God is merciful toward me, a sinner."

My note-taking continued in the midst of his silence.

After some time, Hal turned and studied me, his eyes peering deeply. His voice began to waver as emotions surfaced. It caught me by surprise.

"I've been struggling for quite a while," he began. "I'm not sure where God wants me to go with my life, how I find the purpose God has in mind for me. It has been gnawing away at me. It seems the more I try to do the things I think God would be pleased with, the more confused I become. It's like I'm going through all the motions of doing the right things, but I still don't know if this is what God wants me to be doing. Sometimes I think it is. But then I feel empty. Going through the motions, but not sure this is what God wants. It's almost like there is something more, and I don't know what it is.

"And I don't even know why I'm sharing this with you, a complete stranger."

I was as surprised as he was. Silence filled the space between us – an uncomfortable silence.

I closed the notebook.

"You know, Hal, I don't have answers either," I reflected.

"You're only the fourth person in this *Query* journey, and I don't have a clue what God has in mind. I don't know how long this journey will last or where it will take me. All I know is, it's before me to ask the question and then listen.

"But your story, how you are living the faith, is powerful. Just listening to your story gives me hope."

We sat quietly for a while, both in thought.

"A couple things come to me, Hal," I continued. "I don't know that they mean anything, but here's what they are.

"First, the very fact that you are struggling ... that you're wrestling ... is good. Perhaps it means the Holy Spirit is inside ... nudging, pushing, discomforting. That is good news. Seems to me, when we feel the most discomforted, that's when God is at work. So, as odd as this sounds, maybe you can give thanks for the struggle because it is evidence that the Holy Spirit is at work in you.

"Second, in my own journey when things seem unclear, the words of the Old Testament prophet Habakkuk have brought comfort in the midst of the discomfort. Somewhere in that book, the prophet says something like, 'If the vision tarries, wait ... it will surely come.' While he was probably talking to Israel, those words speak to me. When I reflect on the things that have caused me past distress, a solution unfolded in time. So, maybe there is comfort in the certainty that at the right time, you will know.

"In the middle of my own marital difficulties, I was searching for answers. It was a heart-wrenching search, and I was uncertain whether I would know the right answer when it came. Then my therapist said, "You'll know when you know." At the time, his counsel ticked me off.

"But he was right. 'If the vision tarries, wait; it will surely come.'"

After a bit, Hal's demeanor changed. He grew excited. It was as though a switch had been thrown. He shared ideas of some not-for-profit business startups that have been rattling around for 'when I get time':

1. TechHelp.net ... providing personal technical support to folks, relying on his engineering expertise;
2. MissionHelp.net ... assisting Christian missions, however he can; and
3. HikeHelp.net ... a hiking/backpacking service, helping others who share his love for wilderness.

"You may be right," Hal reflected. "Maybe this is the nudge I've needed. Maybe the vision has been before me all the time and I just couldn't see it."

As they strolled down the hallway of the San Jose airport with his arm around her waist, Hal was animated. Yva seemed to hang on his every word.

A story shared ... a blessing received.

Empty

"O Lord, my heart is not lifted up, my eyes are not raised too high;
I do not occupy myself with things too great and too marvelous for me."
Psalm 131:1 (NRSV)

It was lunchtime at Wendy's; we were several tables apart. A lone middle-aged African American woman with her back toward me, she was following the beat of the background music coming from the ceiling speakers. A music lover, perhaps?

"You must enjoy music. I've been watching you tapping your toes," I smiled and said as I passed by on my way to the trash can. She looked up, with twinkling eyes behind the glasses. "Oh, yes I do!" she giggled.

"Any special kind of music?"

"Oh, I love gospel music! Any music, as long as it's gospel."

"Ah, so you're a woman of faith."

Extending my hand, I began. "My name is Larry," and she took mine. "I'm Oleisha," she said, as the smile continued. She listened with interest to the explanation of *The Query*, and offered the empty chair so conversation could unfold.

"Well," she said, "I've just come from the dentist, so I'm a little woozy. But, sure, this sounds interesting and I'm not in a hurry."

Her story began to unfold.

Oleisha was raised in the San Francisco Bay Area in a large family of seven children, she the third oldest. Her dad was military, so they moved around. Wherever they were living, her mom insisted they go to church, and Baptist became the norm. "Mom is still in the Bay Area," she said, "but Daddy died a couple months ago. He was 85."

Now a 48-year-old single mom, the center of her life is her 17-year-old son. He's a high school senior in their Sacramento suburb.

Oleisha struggles with high blood pressure and seizures, so she receives disability under SSI. "I try to make a little extra money by cleaning houses, but this economy has hurt. People seem to be doing more of their own housecleaning today than a couple years ago. It makes things pretty tight."

To keep expenses down, she has no car; she relies on public transportation. "That's why I've got some time. Buses to the foothills don't run too often."

I began to explain the source of *The Query* project.

"I don't know a lot about the Bible," she said. "It's just way too confusing for me." She remembered *Old Testament* and *New Testament*, but the name of Peter didn't ring a bell.

"So, Oleisha ... *what is the reason for the hope that is within you?*"

She turned quiet, and took a long pause. Then, she replied very softly, "I don't really know. I don't really have any hope."

We talked for quite a while, in quiet conversation. We talked about –

> Faith ... "it's not an important part of my life."
> Church ... "I haven't been to church in a long, long time."
> Gospel music and singing ... "Yeah, I guess faith may be more important than I think, because the songs mean so much to me."

Oleisha has been reading *The Power Within You*[1].

"Every morning, I look in the mirror and say to myself, 'I love you'. And that helps a lot. But, hope? I don't know. I'd like my life to be better. I'd like to be able to understand people better."

Our conversation was coming to a close. It was time to leave – she to pick up meds at a nearby pharmacy, and me back to the office.

"Thank you," she said, as she took my hand on parting. "Thank you for reminding me of something I've forgotten. Maybe it's time for me to find a church again."

A story shared ... a blessing received.

Footnote:

[1] The *Power Within You*, by Eric Butterworth, HarperCollins Publishers. www.harpercollins.com

Purpose

*"To the penitent, God provides a way back;
he encourages those who are losing hope
and has chosen for them the lot of truth."*
Sirach 17:20 (NAB)

Wearing a Marlboro-man jacket and well-worn dark grey jeans, he was muscular, trim, clean shaven, and tanned. On this 9am flight, his hard-charging style was apparent with his breakfast order: cranberry juice with two vodkas. Surely, here, a character worthy of *The Query*!

We both reveled in the rare privilege of a relaxing flight with an empty center seat and room to spread out. The first vodka went fast. He took a deep breath, opened the second one, and slowed down. A few minutes later, the conversation began.

Karl was engaging and at ease as his story unfolded. A road builder, these days he often finds himself flying back and forth between his Chicago-area home and Ft. Worth where his fiancée works in the 'roll off' disposal business.

"How did a road builder in Illinois meet someone in Ft. Worth?" I asked.

"At a rock concert," he laughed.

When he's not building roads, Karl is passionate about *I Rock the Cause*, a nonprofit which raises the visibility of other nonprofits through rock concerts (see *www.IRocktheCause.org*). As much as business allows, he aids the group any way he can.

They met at a concert in Dallas. "Erica was drop-dead gorgeous, and even though I had decided to take a break from relationships, I couldn't take my eyes off her. So, we started talking. Eight months later, here I am, a long-distance commuter on United!" We both chuckled.

Why had you decided to 'take a break'?

"Well, at 50 and after three marriages, I decided that maybe I needed time to figure out why I can't seem to stay married. I hadn't intended to get back into a serious relationship but, man, she was so beautiful, I just had to find out if maybe she could be the one."

How's it going so far?

"So far, great! She needs me, and maybe I need her. Erica is divorced, and Roman Catholic, and was feeling alone. And recently she's been diagnosed with pancreatic cancer, serious. So, we don't know how long we have.

"I got along pretty well with wives #1 and #2," Karl reflected, "but not with #3. That was a real mistake. Maybe we just weren't really ready for it."

He has four kids – ages 30, 24, 16, and 8 – with joint custody of the youngest, a son, who is in a private Catholic school.

The conversation paused as I reviewed my notes. Then, "Karl, I'm amazed that you've been able to get through three marriages, and now in another relationship. That takes a lot of resilience. Where do you find it?"

"Well, I'm a Christian," he reflected, "and that has helped."

He had been very open in sharing his story, and it seemed to be a good time to pose the query. After explaining the context of 1 Peter 3:15, we continued.

"So, Karl, *what is the reason for the hope within you?*"

He was quiet as he thought it through. Then, very slowly, he began. "It has to do with my kids. I want my kids to have a better life than I did. I guess it's centered in the belief that we can have a better society than the generations before, and that has to start with a handful of people who believe that."

His eyes danced as he shared that *I Rock the Cause* was helping him make that difference – that he had found a way to blend his love for rock music with helping any nonprofit further its cause. "I just try to be a good influence on those who come to our concerts and through that, I hope, with my kids."

It seems Karl has found purpose through his passion for music. Road building provides his livelihood; music fills his soul.

"I'm curious, Karl. What part did faith play in shaping this hope within you?"

He fell silent. Then, slowly he unbuttoned the cuff of his sleeve and scrunched it up to his armpit. A long, ugly scar stretched from the elbow and disappeared under the sleeve.

"Eighteen years ago, I was diagnosed with skin cancer and it was serious. I had been lost, drifting in life. For the first time in my life, I prayed to the Lord and meant it. I asked His forgiveness, and asked for His help. After surgeries and treatment, thanks be to God I am cancer-free. That experience changed me. I'm filled with the conviction to make the world a better place in any way I can, and *I Rock the Cause* is one way for me to do that. Helping nonprofits be successful helps the world."

I probed further. "How is it that you thought of turning to God in prayer at that dark moment?"

"I grew up Congregationalist but it just never seemed to work for me. Eventually I became dissatisfied with the church-of-the-denomination. They just seemed too interested in 'church', and not about faith. I had left church and religion. I can't explain why, but in that moment, I just knew that only God could fill the emptiness. Only God could heal me and fill me."

Today, Karl is a member of a non-denominational church in a Chicago suburb. He claims 'Christian' as his identity.

We had landed at O'Hare, and the bell signaled the flight had ended. He stood, turned with outstretched hand, and said quietly, "Please say a prayer for Erica."

A story shared ... a blessing received.

Secrets

*"You who know our fears and sadness,
grace us with your peace and gladness;
Spirit of all comfort, fill our hearts.
Healer of our every ill, light of each tomorrow,
give us peace beyond our fear,
and hope beyond our sorrow."*
Healer of Our Every Ill, by Marty Haugen[1]

It had been 6 weeks. A month-and-a-half since the Alaska flight.

Why? Why this assignment? Why is it always before me, to ask the question? Why does it persist so?

The morning routine at the office had not been routine. A quick lunch break, early and alone, would help. It was a typical late morning in midsummer Sacramento. In a couple hours, the heat would become uncomfortable before the late-afternoon delta breeze kicked in. Rubio's Fresh Mexican Grill on Marconi Avenue was just the spot, with an outdoor patio and large thatched umbrellas for shade.

Nearing the end of a relaxing lunch, my wandering thoughts were interrupted with a question: *Who does God have in mind for The Query today?* Or maybe a rest today. That would be nice!

He was sitting alone at the next table, had been there before me. He finished his lunch, gathered the cup and burrito wrapper, and walked to the trash. Ah, great … I'm off the hook.

Then he about-faced, walked back to his table, and sat quietly in the shade of the thatch umbrella. I gathered my courage and turned to engage. But before I could make contact he rose, walked to his car, and drove away. Off the hook after all – until I glanced around.

She was sitting at the table behind me, facing the other way, which is why I hadn't noticed her. Dressed business casual with a cell phone ear piece, she was reading a book while nibbling at lunch. She appeared to be in her fifties, of average height, with auburn blonde hair.

"Pardon me," I interrupted. She looked up. "This will seem odd, I know, but I have a favor to ask. I'm working on something which I'm sure will end up being a book. It involves a question, and I've learned that it works best with a complete stranger."

She was attentive, but guarded. "Let me give you my card, so you'll know who I am," as I reached for my wallet. But, no business card. The only card was from a couple years earlier of my volunteer leadership role in the regional church body of my tradition. "My name is Larry," I said, placing the card in her hand.

She sat for a moment, reading the card. Then, "Lutherans and Catholics don't get along," she said quietly, and returned the card.

"So you're Catholic?"

"Since the day I was born, but I wouldn't say I'm Catholic," she replied.

"Oh. Well, would it be fair to say you're Christian?" I parried.

"No," she replied quickly. "It would be fair to say I'm spiritual. I'm not religious."

"Wonderful," I said, as I extended my hand. "My name's Larry," I repeated.

"I'm Mary," she replied as she took my hand.

"Mmmm ... Mary! That's a nice Catholic name," I smiled, and so did she. "May I sit, and explain the project?"

"Sure," as she nodded to the empty chair. "How long will this take?"

I explained that I was early in the project, and so would be grateful for however long she might have, but that it seemed to be about 20 minutes depending on how talkative she might be. "Ok," Mary said, "it sounds interesting, and maybe better than this book I'm slogging through." It was a book related to her work about technical sales in a local industry.

I asked if she was familiar with Peter, a disciple of Jesus. She was. I shared the struggle I'd had with 1 Peter 3:15, the uncertainty of not knowing how to reply should someone ask me the question, and the relief in that moment when my breakfast buddies observed that it would be highly unlikely anyone ever would.

That brought a chuckle. "Well," Mary said, "don't be so sure. It could be at the moment you least expect it, someone sits down beside you and asks precisely that question. It could happen." She said it with a smile that almost seemed a challenge.

"Yes, I guess it could," I acknowledged, "but not you, Mary, because that's my job today." She smiled. "I get to ask the questions. So, here we go: *what is the reason for the hope that is within you?*"

Mary sat silently for a moment. Then, with a determined stare, she declared, "I don't have any hope." She fell quiet, staring at me – almost with an air of satisfaction in her declaration, awaiting my reaction.

I looked at her quietly. "Hmmmm. This may surprise you, Mary," I said, "but this isn't the first time I've heard that – so you're not alone."

She did seem surprised, and a little taken aback.

"Tell me what's behind that."

Mary looked deeply into my eyes. Then, in a firm but quiet voice, she said, "The string to that balloon was cut when my 6-year-old grandson was diagnosed with leukemia."

We both sat silently for a moment.

"Oh my," I sighed. "I'm so sorry. But I'd like to know more."

And so, Mary's story unfolded. The more she shared, the deeper my understanding of a life in which hope had been lost. She is a native Californian and grew up in a farming community in the central valley. Eventually the family moved to Redding.

She hesitated. "I had an OK childhood," she continued, "except that when I was 8, I was sexually molested, but not by a family member."

We both paused. I was uncertain how to proceed.

"And then?" I asked quietly.

"My brother was 18 when he was killed by a drunk driver. A couple months later, my mother died of cancer. My dad lived 5 more years. He just couldn't bear the pain of being without Mom.

"Five years after that, my other brother died from a brain aneurysm."

She married a military pilot in 1972. He was shot down over Vietnam, survived, and was rescued. They eventually had two children. "After 20 years of marriage, my husband died from Vietnam injuries. I've been single ever since."

She has several grandchildren, all in the area.

"Mary, I'm not sure when, but at some point, I'd like to reconnect with you after I've had a chance to put on paper what you've shared. I think your story will speak to a lot of people. Can I have your name and address so I can follow up?"

Her response was quick, and pointed. "No. You don't need that information. It doesn't have anything to do with what I have shared."

"Of course, that is true," I acknowledged, "but I just want to make sure I've captured things the way you shared. How may I get in touch with you?"

"Mary. Just say Mary. That must do." She was resolute.

"Ok," I agreed. "Let me take a minute to review my notes to make sure I can decipher what I've written." They were written on the back of a Rubio's placemat. She sat patiently.

After a bit, I continued. "Just a couple things, Mary. I can't imagine how awful the experience of a little girl at 8 years of age being sexually molested.

But I'm curious. How did your mom and dad react when you told them about it?"

She stared at me. "I never told them. I couldn't. He was a family friend, and I knew my dad would have killed him. I couldn't tell them."

"Oh my," I sighed. "How did you get help? It must have been awful."

She stared again, and an even longer pause. "I never told anyone. No one. You're the only person I've ever told, and I'm not sure why I told you. And now you know why I won't give you my personal information. I don't want anyone who knows me to know about it."

We sat in silence as I wrote. Then more time to just sit for a bit, with no conversation – just to sit and think. I was at a loss as to what to say. My thoughts were whirling around the place of suffering and, in my experience, especially the place of suffering within the Catholic tradition. I reflected on my own life and how, in comparison, I have been spared such intense suffering. It seemed no wonder that Mary had lost hope.

Softly, the conversation continued. "Mary, I am so sorry. So very sorry. I'm not sure where to go with this, but there is one more question. You began by saying that you were 'spiritual' and not religious." I paused. "What does that mean to you, so that I understand?"

She looked across the table at me with a surprising tenderness.

"Are you familiar with the 12-step program?" she asked. I responded that I am. "Then you know about the concept of a higher power. I don't know if there is a God. I have wrestled with that for a long time. But I do believe that there is a power greater than us that created all this (as she swept her hand to the natural beauty of the day), who wants us to enjoy it and love in return.

"People say that each life experience is supposed to open the door and teach you something, and I'm not alone in that thinking. But sometimes you need to lay down the pencil and quit taking the test. That's me. I just want to put down the pencil and quit taking the test."

She fell silent.

After a moment, I continued. "What about your grandson, Mary. Did he die?"

"Oh, no," she smiled, as she stood up. "He's fine!"

Mary walked to her car and drove away. I remained for a while and soaked up the sun of a beautiful summer day on the patio at Rubio's. And said a prayer for Mary and a prayer of thanks, and went back to work.

A story shared ... a blessing received.

Footnote:

[1] *Healer of Our Every Ill*, by Marty Haugen, (verse 1). © 1987 GIA Publications, Inc. Used with permission.

Rethinking

*"Train a child in the way he should go,
and when he is old he will not turn from it."*
Proverbs 22:6

She was nearing the end of a tuna salad on whole wheat, sitting next to the large window overlooking the entry to Country Club Mall, occasionally glancing at a spiral notebook. It was Friday, lunchtime at La Bou, a popular Sacramento café. She was dressed casually in blue jeans and sandals, with a sweater over a casual shirt.

"Excuse me. I'm in the middle of a book project, and as part of it I ask a few questions of persons I don't know. My name is Larry ... here's my card."

The Query ...
a book project

Larry D. Moeller
P.O. Box 7163
Maryville TN 37802

querier@risenindeed.com   (865) 984-9040 ext. 110

This would be the initial attempt at introducing myself and the concept with a newly-minted business card declaring: ***The Query ... a book project***. I had been wondering whether explaining the premise as being based on a biblical text was influencing the responses.

It also seemed that stories from complete strangers were genuine and authentic. On the several occasions when engaging with friends or colleagues, each time had proven difficult and ineffectual. The nature of the prior relationship seemed to introduce a bias in the reply, almost a 'this is what I think Larry wants to hear' kind of reply.

"Hello," she replied as she took the card, smiled, and shook my hand. "My name is Mora." Her eyes smiled, too. It seemed like a good start.

"Hello, Mora. Do you have a few minutes?"

She studied the card. "Sure. I'm on my lunch break. What's the book about?"

"Well, as you can see from my card, it has to do with a question. Let me explain. For some time, I've been studying a book. It's a collection of writings by a number of authors. There is a phrase in one of those writings which has stuck with me for a while. I just can't seem to shake it. It says,

Always be prepared to give the answer to the question when someone asks, of the reason for the hope that is within you … and do so with gentleness and respect.

"The reason for the hope within you?" Her eyes were still smiling. "That *is* interesting."

"Yeah, for a while I was kind of worried that someone would come along and ask me that question, and then I'd have to figure out how to answer it. But then I thought, 'what are the odds someone is gonna ask that exact question?', so now I don't worry about it."

She laughed.

"Instead, for the last few months, I've been asking the question – in airplanes, on sidewalks, at restaurants. It's been fascinating, and I've heard some powerful stories."

"I'll bet you have," her smile continued.

"So, that's what the book is about. Those stories. And I was sitting at the table behind you, wondering what the next story might be. So, Mora, let me ask you: *what is the reason for the hope within you?* And if it's ok with you, I'll be making some notes as I listen."

She was silent for a bit, studying my eyes as she thought. Then, her story began with one word.

"God."

She looked at peace with the answer, and content to leave it there.

"Hhmmmm," I replied. "Tell me more."

"I was raised in a religious family. At a young age, we were always looking for what would be best for everybody. I guess to empower people to do the best they can. That has stayed with me, from those early years, so that maybe when I leave this world I will have had as positive an impact on the lives of others as I could.

"It never ends, seems to me. There is no ending answer to the question. We won't ever find the answer, it's just something that's there."

"Thank you, Mora. That was nice," I said. "Tell me a little more about being raised within a religious family. What does that mean?"

"We were raised in a religious belief," she continued. "Christian Scientist, though I'm not part of that now, or any church for that matter, and haven't been for a long time. But it was about healing from within. Thus, my spiritual center: the belief that people can be better than they are."

Mora grew up in the Bay Area with a brother and three sisters. Her dad was a machinist at the Kaiser shipyard. Mom was one of eight children, so a large family seemed normal.

"Mom was determined that we go to church regularly. Dad didn't much care. So, all through my school years, we were in Sunday School. Christian Scientists believe in self-healing, and I believe there is a powerful part of God that can do that. But I also believe that doctors and medicine are on this earth for a purpose, too."

At 18, she married her childhood sweetheart. A couple years later, her dad died (at 55) from a work-related illness. "Mom re-married. She was an alcoholic, and she married an alcoholic. That lasted about a year. She was clean and sober for the last 15 years of her life. But she died of lung cancer 8 years ago. I guess it was from the smoking, a habit she just couldn't kick."

Mora's childhood sweetheart proved to be an abusive man, verbally and physically, so after 13 years the marriage came to an end. Healing began. She fell in love and followed her heart to Sacramento. Her second marriage (now 22 years strong) brought an automatic family of three daughters and a son and now, three grandsons. "By marriage, I guess they're my stepchildren – but to me, they're my kids and my grandkids."

What have been the times when *the reason for the hope within you* has carried you through? What have been the tough times as you look back?

Mora was quiet for a bit. "I lost a sister 10 years ago, to breast cancer. That was tough. And we went through a tough time with our youngest daughter. She's now 31, but she's been in and out of drug rehab since she was 17. Things were rough for a while. She's an alcoholic. She lost custody of her son. I was divorcing her from my life. Her mom was schizophrenic, so maybe there's a connection. But she's in a safe and sober environment now, so maybe things will straighten out."

"Mora," I observed, "it sounds like those early years, when your mom took you to Sunday School so faithfully, proved to have a lasting effect. Where are you today on your faith journey?"

"I guess I'm spiritual, but I'm not engaged in any organized religion. But," she reflected, "I've been very much shaped by it."

As we stood to part, Mora thanked me. "This has been quite a conversation. A very uplifting one. It has caused me to think about things I've lost sight of, kind of like therapy."

"Well," I said, "would it surprise you to learn that the phrase at the start of our conversation comes from the Bible? It's in 1st Peter."

"Really!" she exclaimed. She handed the card back to me. "Would you write it on your card? I want to look it up tonight, and think about this some more."

And so, across the top of her card is scrawled … *1 Peter 3:15*.

A story shared … a blessing received.

Months had passed since the draft of Mora's story had been mailed. Perhaps she had moved and forwarding time of the postal service had expired. Then, an e-surprise.

Subject: *The Query*
From: "Mora"
Date: Sun, January 12, 2014 5:58 pm
To: querier@risenindeed.com

Hello Larry: I bet you're surprised to hear from me after this long. I lost the letter you sent to me and just recently found it again. I love your book. I think it sounds very hopeful. I wouldn't change anything on my story. I do want to update you on my life events. I now have 4 grandsons and my youngest daughter has been sober for over 3 years and now has her life with her son. I have found a wonderful church that my daughter introduced me too. Since going back to church I feel uplifted about religion and truly found my spirit that my Mother taught me so long ago. I wish you the best in publishing your book *The Query*.

Thanks.

_____, aka Mora

A blessing received, indeed.

Insights: *The Novice*

The grip of the *Deep Compelling* is unshakeable. It opens the door to a journey beyond imagining. Maybe the Quentin experience was beginner's luck. Maybe it was part of some grand orchestration. It doesn't matter. It surely was the start of a journey launched in timidity and clumsiness.

Trusting that the training wheels were firmly anchored, the focus in these early encounters was on technique. On learning to navigate a conversation to the point of posing 'the question', without coming across as a creep or some kind of Bible-thumping social misfit. And wondering all the while whether those training wheels *were* firmly anchored!

My timidity was not a fear of engaging people in conversation. No, it rested with getting to the point of asking the question. *Asking* the question was easy. Getting *to* that point in the conversation – well, that's another matter. The text in 1 Peter is no help. It just says to be ready when the question comes.

So, it was helpful that the *Deep Compelling* was ever present. There was something of a greater purpose here. It wasn't just to engage in idle pleasantries, though at the outset it was unclear what kind of greater purpose might unfold.

I began to watch for circumstances which would allow a conversation of 20 minutes or more. Of course, the added benefit to conversation with a seatmate on a long flight is that he or she has nowhere to go. But the *Deep Compelling* didn't limit its instructive to only that fateful Anchorage-to-Seattle flight. For months – years, actually – it gnawed at me: '*Ask the question.*' Muster the courage in whatever setting, and *ask the question*.

So, the stories *Peace* and *Clarity* were, once again, with captive seatmates. They brought opportunity to practice initiating and guiding conversations to the point of posing the question. Very much the novice, the focus in *Peace* was navigating the conversation. Such single-mindedness overshadowed attention to note taking, to my later dismay, as notes of the conversation with Thom proved regrettably skimpy. Clearly, here was something to learn: how to listen attentively, yet interrupt the flow with respectful pauses for note-taking to catch up.

As had Quentin, Thom gave his contact information for future follow up. His reply to the initial draft of *Peace* was gracious:

> "Your interpersonal gift to probe tactfully is best in class and would make Charlie Rose jealous."

Note-taking improved with *Clarity*. Hal was not put off by the occasional pauses. It seemed the notebook, itself, was serving a useful purpose. It seemed to lend credibility to 'the book project' as being more than idle curiosity. But *Clarity* introduced something beyond guiding the conversation and note taking. Hal shared his deepest vulnerability, and it caught both of us by surprise. It is my natural instinct to suggest a 'fix' to another's dilemma. While always well intended, it sometimes isn't helpful. In the midst of Hal's vulnerability, my instinct fell short. I had no 'fix' to offer. Only silence.

I am neither ashamed nor embarrassed to reveal personal experiences which may put another at ease. But the intertwining of faith with those experiences has not been my practice, in any setting. Perhaps that is a remnant of stoic German roots or rural Midwest piety. No matter. With Hal, for reasons I can't explain, I found myself meeting him at his vulnerability with my own, and faith the common bond. Two complete strangers brought together on an airliner for a purpose neither anticipated nor understood.

I don't know the impact on Hal. But for me, *Clarity* had revealed that my faith foundation was sufficient for this and future encounters with persons unknown to me ... clothed in gentleness and respect.

'Trust the One whose hand is on your shoulder' was just as fitting for me and the discomfort of *The Query* as it had been for Ethan and his new bicycle.

The encounter with Oleisha (*Empty*) was significant in several ways: a) approaching someone in a public setting where passersby may observe; b) initiating the conversation beyond my racial or ethnic comfort zone; and c) preparing for a life story in which faith or hope may be absent.

One problem with the Deep Compelling is that it doesn't go away. Discomfort returns, and trust and surrender follow. It isn't reserved for long flights. After all, passengers on airplanes represent a very small sample of the American demographic. Airfares require financial means, and financial means are often preceded by higher education. Honoring the Deep Compelling means learning to engage in a variety of settings. So, at Wendy's, it was Oleisha.

Oleisha's kind and gentle manner softened her response to the query: "I don't really have any hope." It enabled quiet conversation around church and its place in her family history. Above all, her reply prepared me for Mary's, in *Secrets*.

And *Secrets*? The training wheels had helped me to listen respectfully. To gain confidence in probing gently for understanding. To keep an even keel when life stories seem grim.

But something about my approach had been bothering me. And so the change of tactic in *Rethinking*, with Mora the test case. The introductory business card made approaching her, a complete stranger, much easier. With Mora, as with all who followed, the phrase *The Query ... a book project* triggered her curiosity to learn more. And the rephrasing of the foundational premise as being derived from 'a book which is a collection of writings by a number of authors' avoided any predisposition to religiosity, or the Bible, or faith.

Mora was at ease as she began to share her story, with a sense of flattery that someone might be interested.

The instinct to probe the role of faith in shaping her life values and her reason for hope was spur of the moment, mostly coming from my genuine curiosity. These three techniques – 1) the introductory card, 2) the premise as from a collection of writings, and 3) the subsequent probing the role of faith as an influence in one's life – became matter of fact over time.

The training wheels could come off.

It's all about balance.

III. Brief Encounters

Four-year-olds don't hide disappointment well.

"Come on, Grampa," he whined. "We haven't gone very far. Can't we keep going?" The training wheels were gone, his confidence growing with every ride.

"No," I replied. "Sometimes things happen we don't expect. There will be other days for longer rides. But not today."

"Why not today?" he cried.

"Every ride is special, Ethan. Even short ones."

Brief Encounters illustrate that while circumstance may dictate brief interaction, there is reason for hope.

Separation	67
Parental Pride	71
Larger Purpose	73
Jury Duty	75
Potential	78
Insights: *Brief Encounters*	82

Separation

*"Good-bye," said the fox. "Here is my secret.
It's quite simple: One sees clearly only with the heart.
Anything essential is invisible to the eyes."*
The Little Prince, by Antoine de Saint-Exupéry[1]

Some tasks are necessary in ordinary life, and this was one of those. On a crisp Saturday morning in October, a trip to the car dealership. The oil change had been put off too long. That 'alert' reminder had become the annoying and persistent warning light, now with a beep that could no longer be ignored. Midweek travel schedules had prevented the usual maintenance drop off.

She appeared to be mid-thirties, petite, with well-tended flowing dark hair, wearing jeans and a sweatshirt. Nestled in her lap, the thick hard-cover book was open midway through. She was immersed in it, oblivious to the customer lounge around her. An empty waiting room chair separated us. The local newspaper and its crossword puzzle beckoned, usually reserved for a part of my evening routine.

She laid the book aside on the chair between us and rose to grab a cup of coffee from the kiosk across the room. Aha, it was the latest in the *Harry Potter* series that had her transfixed!

"Oh, yes," she smiled as she sat down and reclaimed it. "I'm a huge fan. This is the seventh one, and I confess I've read them all. I decided to read one when my daughter did and have been hooked ever since." We shared the sentiment of admiration for the imagination and story-telling skill of J.K. Rowling.

"How old is your daughter?"

"She's 16 now, but she began reading them when the first one came out. We both did."

I shared that I had become more appreciative of the challenge of writing a book, and gave her *The Query ... a book project* card. She studied it closely. "What's the book about?"

I explained the fascination with another book, its compilation of writings of many authors, and the admonition by one of the authors to *'always be prepared to give the answer to the question, if someone asks, of the reason for the hope that is within you ... and to do so with gentleness and respect.'* And that I'd been asking the question and gathering stories at those times and in those places where time was not a problem.

She was intrigued. "Who do you ask?" she said.

"It seems to work best with complete strangers. People I don't know, and who don't know me. Like on long airplane flights. Or at a lunch table in a restaurant. Or maybe even in a customer lounge at a car dealership," I smiled.

Her curiosity kicked in. "You mean, me?"

"It's too early to do the crossword puzzle, anyway," I replied, laying aside the newspaper. I'd learned to keep the Moleskine© with me, and so reached into my backpack. She was intrigued to see the handwritten notes with story after story filling the pages.

"How does it work?" she asked.

I described how the process has been unfolding as I learn, usually beginning with just listening to the story of their lives and making notes along the way.

"I haven't talked with a *Harry Potter* fan yet. Do you have the time?"

"How long does it take to flush a radiator?" she joked.

She took my extended hand of introduction. "My name is Hannah," she replied.

Hannah. How that name seemed to complement her personality: warm, accepting, present in the moment.

Hannah grew up in the Philippines, one of six children with a large extended family. Every weekend would be spent with her brothers and sisters and twenty-seven cousins. After earning a BA degree at 22 in international studies, she and her mom and dad emigrated to the United

States in 1989, leaving the five younger siblings behind with an uncle to care for them. "The country was a mess. There was all kinds of upheaval and change as the time of Ferdinand Marcos came to an end."

Leaving was the right thing to do, she intimated. The economy was in shambles; cronyism and nepotism was rampant throughout the government. Opportunities were in the United States.

But it was difficult. In time, her father returned to the Philippines, leaving her and her mom behind. "Mom and Dad have been separated for 15 years – not divorced, but separated. He began a second family in the Philippines and lives with them. We don't see him."

For a long time in those days, she struggled. "Why am I here? What are we doing here?" were questions she couldn't escape.

She married. A daughter came along, as did an eighteen-year career in data management with a multi-billion-dollar company. But the marriage didn't last, and they separated when her daughter was 5. She shares custody with the dad, who lives in the Pacific Northwest. Her daughter, a sophomore, attends a private Catholic school.

"I grew up Roman Catholic. In the Philippines, that was normal. There is a small minority of Muslims, but most people are Catholic."

What about your brothers and sisters? Where are they?

"Two of my sisters live in the Bay Area, and we see each other occasionally. The others remained in the Philippines. We don't see them."

Our conversation turned to the query.

"The divorce was hard on me," Hannah said softly. "Do I have hope? Yes, because I believe that things happen for a reason, and sometimes it is the little things which help get you through."

A four-year relationship recently ended, when he died. "It's only been a month. Our families have been grieving together.

"Maybe being raised Roman Catholic has helped me to feel that there is always hope, every day. I try to stay close to that," she reflected, "but even so, I'm burdened carrying my cross."

The pain overshadowed her for a bit. She turned silent, reflecting.

Then, "That's interesting, *The Query*. In college, when I was 18, we had to read Antoine de Saint-Exupéry's book, *The Little Prince*. That has been a book about hope, for me. It has given me direction, a light at the end of the tunnel. It reminds me that one mark of humanity is kindness." Today, at age 42, *The Little Prince* brings her peaceful thoughts and a reminder of hope.

"Hannah, your car is done," the intercom interrupted.

And so was her story.

A single mom, off to tend to her daughter ... to her grieving ... to her living.

A story shared ... a blessing received.

Footnote:

[1] *The Little Prince*, by Antoine de Saint-Exupéry. Copyright 1943 by Harcourt, Inc. Copyright renewed 1971 by Consuelo de Saint-Exupéry. English translation copyright © 2000 by Richard Howard. Houghton Mifflin Harcourt Publishing Company, 215 Park Avenue South, New York, New York 10003.

Parental Pride

"Give us joy to balance our affliction for the years when we knew misfortune."
Psalm 90:15[1]

She was smiling as her fingers flew across the smart phone, texting away. The smile complemented her blonde hair and a warm, gracious face. She laid the phone aside and began to clear her table. Lunch hour was winding down at La Bou, the popular Sacramento bistro.

Nan received my introductory card and extended her hand warmly, along with an invitation to the empty chair alongside. She was intrigued by the unfolding book project.

At 18, she left her Bay Area home for Sacramento to attend college. In three weeks, at age 23, comes graduation and an intercultural communications degree. With a specialty and skill as an American Sign Language interpreter, Nan is excited at the prospects ahead. Teaching in an after-school program has cemented a love of learning which has shaped her sense of the future. She hopes to teach in high school, or interpret lectures for college professors.

"My mom passed away when I was 6," she related. "She was a nurse, and got pricked by a dirty needle at work. Shortly after, she was diagnosed with AIDS and lived for 8 years. Early on, me and my sister came along, and neither of us have tested positive – but it was hard on us, and especially on Dad.

"As I said, I was 6. My sister was 3. The first year was hard for me. Today, I guess I see it as mourning, or grieving. At the time, all I know was that I missed Mommy. For Dad, though, it took a lot longer. I think he grieved for at least five years, and maybe he still isn't over the loss.

"Dad gave up everything in his life to care for us, which is why I'll do anything for him. He kept telling us that things would get better, that everything happens for a reason.

"After my mom died, I guess you could say that we were very religious. We went to Mass with Dad every Sunday. Eventually he remarried in the

Catholic church, to my step-mom. She is Greek Orthodox. So, I was raised in the Catholic church. But after elementary school, I fell away from church and haven't returned. I don't know why. I just haven't."

The conversation turned to the query, and her reason for hope.

"I know there is something higher than us, that there is something to look forward to. I guess that comes from my faith. My grandma, Dad's mom, was very religious. She was Roman Catholic, too."

She paused for a moment, in thought. Then, "I guess my hope is to be successful and make my parents proud. To have faith in myself."

Class beckoned, and so we parted. And though parting with smiles, I wish there had been more time.

A story shared ... a blessing received.

Footnote:

[1] a paraphrase of the morning psalm in *Magnificat*, November 19, 2013. *Magnificat*, PO Box 822, Yonkers NY 10702. 1-866-273-5215. www.magnificat.com.

Larger Purpose

*"Now hope that sees for itself is not hope. For who hopes for what one sees?
But if we hope for what we do not see, we wait with endurance."*
Romans 8:24-25 (NAB)

Las Vegas is a common connection on Southwest Airlines when heading to the eastern U.S. from Sacramento. It was Christmas Eve. She was Midwest bound for the holidays; I, the East Coast.

She was twenty-something with a firm handshake and an engaging smile. Behind the smile was a self-confidence which was refreshing. And so, though the time would be short, out came the notebook and the introductory card.

Laura was intrigued by *The Query* project, and open to sharing.

After 4 years of active duty in the U.S. Air Force, she opted for the reserves and college. "I'm 25 and studying microbiology up north," she shared. She met her boyfriend in the Air Force. They're now in college together.

She paused to reflect on the query: *what is the reason for the hope that is within you?*

"My boyfriend and I have been wondering about our purpose, our future. We're not sure where things may lead.

"I feel I'm destined to do something really big, but I'm not sure what it is. It just feels like I should be able to help people. I'm not to be selfish, and I'm to give everything possible I can give. I haven't figured out how I go about doing it, or when. All I know is, I care about other people more than I care about myself."

She was earnest. She spoke with conviction of a larger purpose ahead.

"Most people don't have that kind of 'big picture' certainty, Laura," I noted. "What shaped you? How has this conviction been formed in you?"

"Oh, that's easy," she smiled. "My two older brothers have always been a big influence in my life. They're always helping others in need, but they're very humble themselves. And my older brother – well, he can talk with anybody. He makes everybody feel like a friend."

Clearly, I thought, some of that has rubbed off on Laura. She is refreshingly outgoing.

"What about faith? Has faith played a part in shaping you or your brothers?"

"Not really. Faith hasn't been a big part of my life. Growing up, we weren't very religious. Mom was Catholic, and so as kids we went to a church now and then. But I stopped after a while. It just didn't do anything for me.

"In high school, I went to a Lutheran church because some of my friends went and there were always fun things going on. I was baptized there, in high school.

"But I can't really say I'm a full Catholic or a full Lutheran.

"I've been waiting for some clarity on the whole faith thing. That's a part of my quest, to gain understanding. I know I do believe there is a higher power, but I don't think I can go to church to get forgiveness for me. That is within myself."

It was a short hop on Christmas Eve, made shorter by a warm smile and thoughtful conversation.

A story shared ... a blessing received.

Jury Duty

"The sun'll come out tomorrow.
Bet your bottom dollar that tomorrow, there'll be sun!"
'Tomorrow', from *Annie*
(the Broadway musical)

It is one of those civic duties which never seem to come at a convenient time. Of course, everyone embraces the privilege and obligation of jury duty. Even so, wouldn't it be great if we could pick when we serve?

The room was overflowing. Rows upon rows of chairs were filled, as were the benches that lined the hall. At least Sacramento County does one thing right: if you're not picked for a jury on the day you report, you're deemed to have served and are excused until the next cycle.

So, elbow to elbow, an overstuffed assembly room of citizens prepared to wait through the day, each hoping to be skipped over. She was leafing through a tattered *People* magazine from the rack against the wall. "I forgot to bring a book," she sighed. "This is going to get old pretty fast."

"Well," I began, "since we're stuck here for a while, maybe it's a good time for the book project I'm working on." I retrieved the ever-present notebook from my backpack. She studied *The Query* card and listened with interest as I explained the premise and process. She was fascinated as we skimmed the handwritten pages of peoples' stories, and smiled as I wrote the date and 'Sacramento County Jury Assembly Room 203' across the top of the next empty page. It was her turn.

"Okay," the smile continued, "but I'm not sure there's much of a story here."

Krista has lived in the Sacramento area for 20 years and works the night shift in an adult assisted-living community. Her husband, Vern, is a tech whiz. Together they're raising two children, ages 6 and 1.

"Dad grew up in Georgia, and my mom in Arkansas. I don't know how they met. He was in the military, and we moved a lot. He was stationed in

Alabama, then Georgia, Arkansas, and eventually California. I'm a military brat. I didn't have brothers or sisters. It was just me."

They divorced when she was 9; she stayed with her dad. He was in his fifties when he died of heart failure. "Military life was hard on Dad. He smoked and drank a lot." She lost touch with her mom after he passed away.

Krista and Vern were classmates in junior high, and attended the same high school. "Vern has a brother and a sister. His mom had a lot of brothers and sisters, and she lives nearby. We visit her almost every day, and she often babysits the kids."

What is the reason for the hope that is within you?

"I guess it would be my children. Once I'm gone, I hope I've done my job and that they'll have a happy life."

What about before the children came along? Did you have hope?

She turned reflective. "I hoped I'd done everything I wanted to do, with no regrets. And I have no regrets. A lot of people call me an optimist. That just comes from my heart."

Her outlook was shaped by her dad. "I think he was pretty proud of me. My father never talked much. But when he did, it counted.

"I respected him, and I still do. When my parents divorced, he gave my mother everything except me. She got it all: material, financial. We started over completely, just me and him. A single father in the military, and he went back to school. He was a person whose actions truly spoke louder than his words."

What about faith?

"My grandmother on Mom's side was very religious. She was always singing. And every night when she would go into her room, she would pray before she went to bed."

And you?

"There are certain times when you go through a rough patch, and you talk out loud. You know, you say things and sometimes they come true. In talking to God, it's sort of like on a TV show: "Ok, God, I'm gonna talk to you now."

"I've always believed that things would always get better. That there's a balance in life, that there's a cycle. It's better to go with the flow, because usually the result is going to be the result. It might be good or bad, and it may not be what you want. But it's usually what you need at the time."

Has church been a part of that?

"We hardly ever went to church when I was growing up. And Vern isn't religious. His mom was Buddhist, but not particularly religious. They didn't go to temple."

The loudspeaker interrupted. "When your name is called, report immediately to Courtroom 3B."

Krista's was third on the list of forty called. She hurriedly gathered her things, and we exchanged goodbyes. "I wish we could have had more time," she said, with an earnest look in her eyes. We parted.

I sat for a while and reflected on Krista. A very kind, pleasant young woman. A young woman who senses a feeling of fate grounded in goodness.

Later announcements didn't include my name. As the day drew to a close, my jury duty was over. But it was different this time.

A story shared ... a blessing received.

Potential

*"He who confers benefits will be amply enriched,
and he who refreshes others will himself be refreshed."*
Proverbs 11:25 (NAB)

Dierdre had just wrapped up her second year of teaching science in the high school of a small town in the upper Midwest. Her contract had been renewed for a third year, and she was excited!

"I'm on my way to the West Coast to meet a college friend. We're going to drive her car from Los Angeles to Seattle on the Pacific Coast Highway and camp along the way. No lesson plans, no agenda. Just whatever comes. That's going to be my summer!"

Dierdre is 24. She was raised by a single mom who never married. "I never knew my dad." There were no brothers or sisters. She grew up in a small rural town, "four houses down from Grandma and Grandpa." Her high school class had 52 students; she was the valedictorian. Because of scholarships, she was able to earn a degree from a private liberal arts college.

"Mom was the oldest of four biological kids. Grandpa worked for the State department, and he had numerous overseas assignments. Mom was 2 when Grandpa got his first overseas post; her brother was born in Europe." Eventually, her grandparents adopted three nieces and nephews, "so there were seven kids in my mom's family growing up."

"Mom and I have a good relationship. She's worked at a call center in the city for a number of years. She served in the Army reserves for over twenty years, was in Desert Storm (under President George H. W. Bush) for a year, and retired from the military. Mom said all she did was drive stick-shift trucks," she smiled.

Is there a special someone in your life? "Oh, no!" she exclaimed. "Guys take too much work!"

What about church, about faith? Has it played a part in your life? "My grandparents didn't really go to church much, but when they did it was Methodist. I believe in God, but I'm not religious."

What is the reason for the hope in your life?

"I guess that would be 'potential'. That's what the reason for my hope is. I see potential for my students, for technological advances. 'Potential' is the reason for the hope within me.

"There is always a bright side, but it's just kind of hard to find it sometimes. I'm an optimist. I get that from my mom and my grandparents."

Dierdre said she has minimal familiarity with or interest in outside current events. She doesn't read a newspaper, though occasionally goes online to check news but with no regular pattern. "I really don't pay much attention to that."

Are you hopeful for the direction of the United States? "Not as much now as I was a few years ago. I wish politicians would do more about what they know to be right and less about what is 'politically correct'. They seem to have no convictions."

What would be a change which would make you more hopeful? "Politicians who are concerned for the future of the country, not just their re-election. Willing to push for more tolerance."

Can you cite an example?

"Sure – gay rights. My students don't see the big deal with gay marriage. They seem to think that as long as it doesn't hurt them (the students), we shouldn't interfere."

Tell me a little about teaching in a small town in the Midwest. What is it like? What is a typical income for a teacher where you live?

"Starting teachers make in the $30,000 range, depending on the size of the school district.

"I teach ninth through twelfth grades, all the sciences: chemistry, advanced chemistry, physical science. Last year, I had six seniors. During a typical day, I get to the office between 7:00 a.m. and 7:30 a.m. The first class starts at 8:10 a.m., and I'm usually home sometime between 7:00 p.m. – 7:30 p.m. I don't do any teacher work at home. I like to leave it all at the school."

There are eight classroom periods a day. She has six classes, one study hall, and one period for prep time. "A year ago, I sponsored a 'mock trial' team after school, but not this year. There just wasn't enough interest."

What's ahead for you, say, ten years out? "I haven't really thought about that. But I would like to be teaching in the same district. I like getting to know the families."

Can you think of a senior student who stood out, who excelled?

"Oh, yes," her face lit up. "Brad took chemistry and advanced chemistry in the same term, and got A's in both. He was very driven, a hard worker. He plans to go into veterinary medicine."

What about an underperformer?

"That would-be Nick. All his shortcomings were always someone else's fault. He's capable, but just doesn't apply himself. I just couldn't seem to connect with him."

What is the ethnic or racial mix of the kids?

"Like the area around us, it's predominately white with less than 5% Hispanic. There are no blacks. There is a large chicken processing plant about forty miles away, and probably half their workers are Hispanic. But we must be too far away to have any of their kids."

What is the place of church in the culture in your small town?

"People go to church, but it seems like it's mostly for show. You would think that their behaviors would be better."

You mean they're sinners?

"Well, I guess we're all sinners," she laughed.

If there are youth activities in the churches, she doesn't hear kids talking about them.

We talked of vocation, and vocation as a calling. "Teaching is my calling. I know it's what I'm supposed to do."

A story shared ... a blessing received.

Insights: *Brief Encounters*

In time and with practice, the gathering of stories comprising *The Query* became enjoyable and deeply rewarding. Sometimes circumstance dictated a brief encounter, as the stories in this section illustrate. Though brief, each encounter was worthy.

Maybe 'always be prepared to *ask* the question' is of significance in brief encounters. Each encounter, each story, is revealing. So, ask the question. Always ask.

Yet, the experience of *Potential* was unique. Its brevity was not due to circumstance. Dierdre and I were, after all, seatmates on a three-hour flight which normally would afford ample time for in-depth conversation. But that proved not to be so.

Maybe she was tired. Maybe I was tired. Or maybe I was just off my game. Regardless, the interaction seemed stilted. Of course, common courtesies were extended. We were, after all, Midwesterners. But the conversation didn't flow easily. Toward the end, Dierdre's passion and enthusiasm surfaced as she spoke of the two students, Brad and Nick. But the anecdotes were brief.

It wasn't technique. By this time in *The Query* journey, a couple dozen stories had been gathered. No, techniques had been honed. Conversations flowed easily. Maybe this was just the first experience where someone was simply reluctant to engage at a deep level. So far in the journey, it has proven to be the only one.

So, why this brief section: *Brief Encounters*?

To illustrate that some encounters may be short lived, either through circumstance or psychology. No matter.

"Every ride is special, Ethan. Even short ones."

IV. *Listening*

It had been several months since his fifth birthday and the arrival of the sleek, black intermediate bicycle with neon-green detail. Gone the red toddler bike with the bald tires. As skills improved, Ethan reveled in the long rides.

"Not that way, Grampa," he hollered, as the hill loomed ahead. "It's too hard." So, we took the long way around.

Long rides are fun when the way is easy.

- - - - - - - - - - - - - - - -

Listening shares the simple joy of listening as stories unfold with memorable twists and turns.

Invasive Love	85
Two-by-Four	92
Favorites	101
Unresolved	106
Principled Living	110
Everything Changed	117
Balance	123
Physics + Astrology	130
Broken Trust	135
Insights: *Listening*	**142**

Invasive Love

*"Honor your father and your mother,
so that your days may be long in the land
that the Lord your God is giving you."*
Exodus 20:12

Immigration is a thread in the fabric of most American families. For many it is an obscure bit of family lore from generations past.

Not so, Teresa. Her dad was born in Mexico, orphaned and adopted early on. "When he was 12," her story unfolded, "his father died. His mom was in a wheelchair. So, to provide for his mom, he got a job picking crops.

"My mom left Mexico in the '70s and came to the San Fernando Valley where she picked oranges in the citrus groves. Eventually she moved north to the Bay Area and got a job working in a candy factory. Later, she cleaned dorm rooms at a university. That was followed by a job at a motherboard assembly plant in the Silicon Valley."

They met in the South Bay, married, and saved to buy a home. Not long after, along came Teresa. "I'm the oldest of four, with two sisters and a brother," she said. When she entered high school, her mom had knee surgery and became a stay-at-home mom.

After undergraduate studies at UC/Berkeley in genetics and plant biology, she transferred to UC/Davis in pre-med. She has applied to medical schools and is in the middle of the selection process. Her applications to the universities of Iowa, Southern California, Davis, and Michigan have been favorably received. Now it's a matter of evaluating and deciding. "They're evaluating me, and I'm trying to decide which one would be the best program and the best fit for me. The California schools would be an easy adjustment but I think I'm ready for more of a change, learning and living somewhere else."

Today, Teresa is on her way to Ann Arbor for an interview with the admissions board. "Yeah, I'm a little nervous," she fidgeted. "But I'm glad I've already done this a couple times. The medical school at the University of Michigan is one of the best, so I hope I do well." She wants to enroll somewhere in the fall.

We chatted about her interviewing experiences. I couldn't help but offer a few tips, since interviews are a part of my everyday world. "Gosh, I wish we'd met a few months ago!' she exclaimed.

I had earlier explained *The Query* project and given Teresa my card, so she watched quietly as the note writing caught up.

Why genetics and plant biology?

"Oh, that was easy," she smiled. "I loved biology in high school. I'd get so excited talking about it at the supper table, Mom and Dad would get as excited as me! They always wanted to hear about my classes and what I was learning. My sisters and brother, on the other hand ..." and we both laughed.

What was the supper table like in your home?

"The table is the center of family. It's where everything is shared, everything comes out. In our home, nothing is secret for long." Her face was glowing. "Mom and Dad are so proud of us, and we're so proud of them. I've been blessed. And I miss them."

You're bilingual, then?

"Si," she laughed. "We spoke only Spanish at home. Mom and Dad both speak English pretty well, but it's in Spanish that the stories are told. It's just easier for them, and for us kids, it's normal."

Well, UC Berkeley, then UC Davis, and now a premier medical school. None of those are cheap. How have you been able to do it?

"Academic scholarships have pretty much paid for everything. My mom was always saying, 'Focus on school. Focus on scholarships.'" Teresa has also received a number of federal grants through the Incentive Awards program.

The conversation turned to another aspect of college life: dating. "Is there someone special?"

As a college freshman, she met Kelvin. "He's my boyfriend," she demurred. And now, four years later, the relationship remains strong. "Kelvin is African American. My parents are kind of traditional, so they didn't meet him until my college graduation ceremony. I introduced him as 'a friend'. My mom knows Kelvin is my boyfriend, but I've not told my dad. I just introduced him to Dad as a friend."

"Our relationship is serious. Kelvin lives in the Bay Area. I've been with him and his family many times. They're very warm and inviting, and welcoming to me as his girlfriend."

"Sounds kind of like *Guess Who's Coming to Dinner* with your mom and dad," I smiled. She was perplexed. "You know," I continued, "that movie from the 60's, starring Sidney Portier, and Spencer Tracy and Katherine Hepburn, about a mixed-race couple."

My age was showing, and we both chuckled. Teresa was not familiar with it, but shared that her relationship with Kelvin is better reflected in the movie *Our Family Wedding*, a more contemporary story of the culture clash of an African American and Latin American relationship.

"My parents' fear, I think – at least my mom's – is not so much a mixed marriage as a diversion from my focus on school."

Kelvin comes from a family with two older siblings, a brother and a sister. "Kelvin is the baby," she smiled. "He and his sister and some girl cousins grew up with his paternal grandmother for a while. He was the only boy in his early years, and then moved back with his mom in middle school. His mom and dad separated when he was young.

"Kelvin's dad reminds me of my dad in his mannerisms and conversations. He is very traditional."

Tell me a little more about your family: your mom, your dad, your growing up years.

"Well, Dad was born in a city in San Luis Potosí, Mexico. Mom was from Apatzingán, in Michoacán de Ocampo. When my grandmother was alive, we would always visit around Christmas time.

"There is a high value placed on family in my culture and that is certainly true for us. Ever since leaving home to go to college, Mom would call me two or three times a day, every day, and always before I went to sleep. She would always check to make sure I had eaten. Now, she texts me. That has helped a lot because it's easier to be connected. I can't always answer right away when she calls, but I can usually reply to a text. Even so, she still calls me at least twice a day, every day."

"How do you feel about that?" I asked. "Does it ever feel like your mom is being invasive in your life? I mean, you're a very attractive young woman. Doesn't it put a cramp in your style?"

Teresa smiled broadly. "No. I understand it."

But how does Kelvin feel about it? Most guys would wonder about a girl whose mother called her several times a day, every day. Does it bother him? Has it affected your relationship?

"Kelvin's family is very different. He talks to his mom maybe weekly, if that. At first he didn't understand. But he's gotten used to it, and he accepts it."

What if you just didn't answer the phone, just let it go to voice mail? Have you tried that? It seems to me at some point, you will want a little more space. How will that happen?

"Oh, my," she sighed. "My mom would go crazy with worry if I didn't answer. I could never do that to her. To me, it isn't that she's being nosy. It's the way she shows her love. For me, it's very powerful to know that my mom cares so deeply. She puts all of us kids ahead of her own needs. It's just the way we are."

What do you think motivates your mom for the frequent contact?

"We've always been a very close family. Every night, while growing up, there would always be a warm 'good night' gesture. 'Everything I do is for my children,' is what mom always says. And she lives that."

Do you ever feel it's an intrusion, or invasive?

"No. It's just Mom knowing what I'm doing, and that I'm ok. It's not an intrusion. If that's invasive love, well, I wouldn't want it any other way."

Sounds like a very precious maternal love.

"Yes," she reflected. "That is probably the best way to describe it. We are very lucky, our family."

The conversation turned. Teresa revealed that the first clash of cultural values in the relationship with Kelvin was her mom's unstated wish for the relationship to end. "I fell in love, and I told Mom I was not going to break up with him. She has accepted it. The phone calls didn't end."

Kelvin is studying marketing in the City. They met through friends at a popular restaurant in Berkeley. "Kelvin seems to be finding his way into marketing as a focus."

What about you? You seem to have a clear idea of what lies ahead for you, purposeful.

"Oh, yes, that would be a good way to describe me. Guided by a purpose. I've had incredible support from family, to be encouraging at the low points when in doubt or tears. My parents always listen, encourage, support. They have all the faith in the world in me."

We sat quietly for a few moments. She had been wonderfully open, and so it seemed a good time to pose the query.

What is the reason for the hope that is within you, Teresa?

She was thoughtful.

"A lot of it is support from family and friends. When I look at where I am, which I don't do often – my mom as a custodial woman, cleaning women's dorm rooms – she told herself that her kids would go to college. When I started kindergarten, she said, 'You're in school to go to college.'

"The support and the love my parents have had for me. They have been a huge value in my life. Whatever I am today, the credit goes to them."

So now you are on your quest to med school. Why medicine?

"I suffered from asthma. The doctors were always very compassionate and understanding. What drives me most is being able to give back. To help the underprivileged. To give back in that way. As a doctor, you're with someone in a very vulnerable time, and I want to be able to help.

"No matter where you start in life, you realize how much potential you do have and with determination and support you can accomplish what you want."

Once again, a pause as note-taking caught up. Then, "Teresa, has faith played a part in this outlook? In this 'shaping'?"

"Oh, yes," she replied, "faith has led me to where I am today. Faith in people themselves is very important. My parents have faith in me. I have faith in them. And their faith in me has instilled a sense of humility."

But what about faith through religion? Is that a factor?

Teresa turned quiet and thoughtful for a moment. "Well, I was brought up Catholic, but I haven't attended church regularly.

"My family is a mixture of culture and religion. If there is a mention of God, it would be with the hope that God will take care of us. When I have doubts, it helps to know that God is taking care of me. At the end of the day, it helps to know that everything happens for a reason.

"Our whole family was 'occasional' church attenders. I'm culturally religious, because the Catholic religion is important in Mexican culture. So when I do attend church, it's a Catholic church. But I don't believe I have to go to church to be spiritual or to connect or communicate with God. That is something you can do anywhere."

And Kelvin?

"Kelvin's mom was very religious. She attended church every Sunday and he had to, too.

"To the extent that religion has shaped me, it is Catholicism, since it is the predominant religion in Mexico. I'm sure it probably had a big influence on my parents even though we didn't go to church that often. But because it is deep in who they are, I guess indirectly it has influenced me."

The flight, and our conversation, had come to an end. It had been delightful.

A story shared ... a blessing received.

Two-by-Four

*"How grateful I am, Lord, for your grace and mercy toward me.
I have no other hope as solid as your will to forgive…"*
An excerpt from the prayer of the day, June 15
Daily Texts 2013[1]

He was immediately friendly. We were three tall men settled into Row 26, his associate on the aisle, and me at the window. At 6'1", I was probably the shortest. His friend on the aisle appeared about my age, maybe a bit younger. My seatmate was distinguished, lean, with thinning hair and glasses, and perhaps in his late sixties.

The latest issue of *The Economist* had my attention during the pre-takeoff routine. Their interaction was light-hearted, jovial, and easy to overhear. He sported a navy blazer and tan slacks; his friend, a navy sweater and tan slacks. It seemed they were on a business trip to Chicago.

Once airborne, I retrieved the several files from my backpack in preparation for the two-day meeting which lay ahead. After a while, he turned to me and our conversation began.

"I'm not nosy," he said, "but I noticed that your paperwork has something to do with the Lutheran church. What takes you to Chicago?"

"I'm going to a meeting a little later today and tomorrow. I serve on the board of the national men's ministry for this piece of the Lutheran church, and we'll be focusing on fundraising."

"Oh, how long will you be in Chicago?"

"I'm returning tomorrow night, catching the 5:15 flight back through Denver on my way home to Sacramento."

"Ah, we'll be on the same flight. We're returning then, too," he smiled.

"Well," I hesitated, "not being nosy, but I happened to overhear some of your conversation, too. You were mentioning something about your church, and a new pastor. What church is that?"

"It's a non-denominational church near Denver. One of those mega-churches."

A mega-church. How many do you worship?

"Oh, we're down a little in the last few years, from about 6,000 on a weekend to about 4,500 now. But I think we're coming back. Maybe it's been the economy."

Is your trip to Chicago church-related, too?

"Oh, no. We're in transportation, and we'll be meeting with a few folks in Chicago to explore some business. Just a quick in-and-out."

Does 'transportation' mean 'moving and storage', like household goods?

"Yep'" he smiled. "Been in it for over thirty years."

It was early January 2011, and the economic downturn had the country in a vise grip. "Well, that business has to have had a rough go the last few years. Not a lot of people moving, with the upside-down housing market. Have you felt the pinch?"

"Oh, yeah," he replied. "It's sort of been a double-punch, with housing and the rising cost of diesel fuel. It's put a lot of the independent haulers in a bind, and we depend on them."

The conversation continued for some time comparing notes on business, the stubbornness of economic recovery, politics. Interestingly, neither of us brought up the most topical news of the day: the shootings in Arizona of Congresswoman Giffords and others. Perhaps we were just weary from the media blitz.

It is always a joy to be seated next to someone who has a zest for living, and my seatmate clearly did. So, it seemed that, rather than preparing for a meeting, it was query time. Out came the notebook and the introductory card.

"Well, it's nice to meet you," I began. "By the way, my name is Larry. In fact, here's my card. If you're open to it, it would be nice if I could ask you a couple of questions as part of a project I'm working on."

He studied the card intently. *"The Query ... a book project,"* he read. "You're writing a book?"

"Well, I think so. Mostly I'm gathering stories, and (opening the notebook) they're all right here."

He was curious as I leafed through the pages of handwritten notes. "Most of them have been on long airplane rides like this one, or in a restaurant, or a customer lounge in a car dealership. Anytime I have an extra hour or so to ask a question, and then just listen."

"That sounds interesting," he said, his eyes a-twinkle. "I'm Stephen. Here's my card," he chuckled. "So, what's *The Query*?"

I explained the basis and the premise, a compilation of writings by a number of authors, a phrase which intrigues me. "And here's the phrase, Stephen: *'always be prepared to answer the question when someone asks of the reason for the hope that is within you ... and do so with gentleness and respect.'* For almost two years now, I've been asking the question and gathering the stories. So, that's the query: w*hat's the reason for the hope that is within you?* But before we get to that, I'd like to know a little more about you so I'll better understand your answer."

And so, the story of Stephen. He had already shared about two sons and a couple grandchildren, because we had done some comparing of families.

Stephen was born in eastern Pennsylvania right after WW II and for the first few years lived on his maternal grandpa's farm of 386 acres. "In that part of Pennsylvania, that's a good-sized farm," he exclaimed. I was curious about his family and siblings, and the idea of growing up on Grandpa's farm.

"I like to say that my family tree is a family bush," he chuckled. "My mom was married twice and so was my dad. Dad's second marriage was to Mom, her first. From Dad's first marriage, I have two brothers and a sister. I'm the only child Mom and Dad had together. Their marriage lasted a couple years. I never knew him growing up.

"Dad was a highly-decorated captain in the Army. He was captured, and spent a couple years in a German POW camp. Just before liberation, he escaped and was seriously wounded. He and Mom met during his recovery in a military hospital in Greenbrier, WV. She was a 'helper' there. I guess Dad was a serious drinker – maybe because of the war injuries, I don't know – but they divorced after a couple years. He died in 1965. I only met him once, the summer before he died."

He paused. "When I was about five, we left Grandpa's farm and moved to Virginia. Mom got a job in DC and met Burt. They married, so from then on I was raised by Mom and Burt, my stepdad. Burt was Jewish, but not a practicing Jew. He didn't go to synagogue, and didn't go with us to church when we went. From their marriage, I have a younger sister."

Did Burt adopt you?

"No, I kept my dad's name," he continued. "Burt's grandfather was a tailor in Russia. He made suits. When the oppression of the Jews by the czar got nasty, his grandfather emigrated to the United States."

Is your mom still alive? "Oh, yes. She's 83 and Burt is 87. They're still married, and they still live in the same DC suburb."

The story turned to him and Wanda, his wife. Her dad, originally from Tennessee, was an Air Force lifer stationed in France. So, Wanda was 'a military brat'. She was born in Texas and her dad's tours took them to California, to England, and eventually to France.

Stephen enlisted in the Air Force and served from 1965-1969.

"Vietnam?" I asked.

No. He served mostly around Europe, wrapping up in France where he met Wanda. They were married under the NATO agreement. "We were married in the village church on Friday the 13th by the mayor, and then married again in the chapel at the base the next day. We've been married 42 years!" he exclaimed.

After the Air Force, they returned to Virginia. Stephen earned a business degree at Georgetown on the GI Bill; Wanda worked part-time while he went to school. They have two sons. The oldest is 34 with a 6-year-old daughter and a 3-year-old son. He is in medical equipment sales and lives near them in Colorado.

The youngest is 27, single, and lives in Los Angeles. He is trying to make it as an actor and appears occasionally in commercials. Both sons graduated from the University of Colorado, where the school mascot is the buffalo. "They like to say they're buffed!" he laughed.

Stephen delighted in sharing the story of his family, of his sons and grandchildren. Here is a man with a zest for living, seasoned by the ways of the world!

The conversation paused, as my fingers and pen caught up. The silence lasted a few minutes as I reflected on his story. It seemed time for the query.

"Thank you, Stephen, for being so open with your story. You have been very gracious. Let's now turn to the query: *what is the reason for the hope within you?*"

He was quiet for a moment. Then, "I know where I'm going, and I know who got me here." Then, more quiet.

The pen was laid aside. "Can you fill that in for me? What does that mean?"

"It took me a lot of years to find out that Christ was the center of my life," he reflected. "I know where I'm going. I'm going to heaven to spend eternity with Christ. So is my wife, and so are my kids. And now we're preparing the grandkids.

"And I know who got me there. Christ paid the price for forgiveness of sins, to open the door to spend eternity with Him. That's His promise, like the old hymn, *Standing on the Promises*. But it took me a lot of years to come to this."

Oh? What do you mean?

Stephen sat quietly for a few moments. "My mom was a Baptist, and she still is. My stepdad was no influence in my faith. As I said, he wasn't a practicing Jew. Church just wasn't something we did together, but it was important to Mom that I go to church, so she got the neighbor to take me. I was baptized at age 12. Mom was there that night, but not Dad.

"But though I was raised a Christian, I fell away. It was while I was in the Air Force that I started to fall away from God, took things into my own hands, made my own direction. It just took a while for my life to really come apart."

Emotion surfaced as his voice hushed. Not a hush of tenderness – no, more of confession. Of humility.

"When I met Wanda in France, she was the oldest of four kids. She took her siblings to church while her mom worked. They lived off base, and she went to a Baptist church.

"After we married, our journey in the faith drifted for a few years. It was my battle with the Lord, not Wanda's. We both just sort of wandered away from church, though she was steadfast in reading Scriptures. We kind of wandered for eight or nine years. That time was woven with business successes, and failures."

I was fascinated. "What were some of the successes?"

"After getting out of the Air Force, we opened a commercial lighting center. It was doing well, and then along came the Arab oil embargo in 1973-74 and everything changed. We shut down the business in 1975, and moved back to Grandpa's farm in the Pennsylvania hills for a couple years. That's where our oldest son was born." The twinkle returned as he continued, "We like to say that he's part hill-billy!"

The time in Pennsylvania was short-lived. A quarrel developed between the heirs to his grandpa's farm, so they returned to Colorado. "With a little one, we tried getting back into church. But that turned sour because I didn't go back with the right spirit. I had been taught that as the husband, I was supposed to be the spiritual leader of the family. I'm not sure that's the way it's supposed to be, but I know I kinda blew the whole thing.

"By 1979, things had really fallen apart. It was a very difficult time. I was completely busted ... mentally, spiritually. Nothing was going the way it was supposed to. I wasn't in control. I moved out and into an apartment.

"After 17 years of marriage, a disastrous separation. During that time, our little boy was the force which kept us in contact with each other. He was my pride and joy," he beamed.

"Then one night about a year later, the Lord got my attention ... with a two-by-four! It was the first week of January in 1980 when I asked Jesus to come into my heart. When I shared with Wanda that I'd asked Christ back into my life, she didn't believe me. She thought it was a ruse. So, she watched me very closely for most of the next year. I know it was the Lord who let her see that I was a changed man.

"It was in late 1979 that my son and I started going back to church. Once I asked Christ back into my life, we went every Sunday. We've been very faithful about church ever since." There was an air of sincerity about him as his story concluded.

I reviewed my notes and reflected on what I had heard, and then turned to continue. "Tell me, Stephen, about that moment when you asked Jesus to come into your life. What was it like?"

He stared at his hands for a moment. "The Lord dropped me on my knees in my living room one night, and it seemed like I could hear him say, 'You messed it up pretty bad'. That got my attention. Of course, I didn't need any convincing. I had messed things up, for sure!"

I was curious, and wondered just how far this could go. "What led to the separation?"

"The world," said Stephen. "I went back to rock and roll, and drinking. A much more 'go-er' life style."

Were there other women?

"Oh, yeah. There were other women. We were separated, and I was just one step from being free!"

Drugs?

"No, never. Even the alcohol was minimal."

Why return to Wanda?

"My grandfather was a man of deep commitment. I was the one going through the rebellion. Deep down, I was always committed to her. But there was a cost to what I did. It took more than a year to overcome the hurt in Wanda's heart. We went to a pastor for counseling. With his help, we turned to a Gary Smalley[2] book, both individually and as a couple."

What's it been like since?

"Well, I know it was the Lord that brought us back together. Now, we're retired. I started a new career in transportation in 1981, went to work for a company, learned the business. In 1989 we bought a small transportation company, grew it, and sold it 3 years ago. Now the Lord is opening the door to start another business with a Chicago company. The guy in the seat next to me is responsible for getting me into the transportation industry 30 years ago."

What prompted you to sell the business?

"Just before the economy crashed, the transportation industry was already feeling the pinch. It didn't take much. When Wall Street collapsed, banks began calling notes on lines of credit. Ours did. They called our notes. Crazy! Suddenly, the banks wanted their credit lines called. We had grown the business to about $6 million. The bank called in their loan of $480,000, and we didn't have the cash to pay it off. So, we prayed, and decided to sell to a business that had the cash. We didn't make anything on the deal, but at least we landed on our feet. And now we're coming up on the end of a 3 year non-compete in the sale agreement. So, it's back into the business we know.

"I want to start a business and bring some of the folks back who have not been able to find work since the sale. It's been a tough time for most of them. I want to do this to build a future for the people who stood with us through the years."

We sat for a bit while I reviewed my notes. I asked more questions, and Stephen filled in the blanks.

"Grandpa was part German, part something else. He was very well-read in the Bible. He was my mentor, and he passed away on June 7, 1971. I was the farm laborer for him. None of his sons wanted to farm." Stephen bought the farm at a sheriff's sale on the courthouse steps in 1994, the result of the squabble of the heirs.

"My grandfather was the biggest influence in my life. Sunday was the Lord's day in his house."

We were approaching the landing at O'Hare. Dutifully the notebook found its way into the backpack, the backpack found its way under the seat ahead, and the tray table returned to its upright and locked position.

Small talk followed. As the plane touched down, Stephen extended his hand. The handshake was warm and genuine. He asked some questions about my history and my family, and I shared. I've become more the listener in this *Query* journey, so I was caught a little by surprise at someone else asking questions. He wrote down the names of my family members, and promised to pray for them.

As he clasped my forearm with a firm goodbye grip, his eyes found mine. He was silent for a moment. Then he said softly, "I've never told anybody my story."

A story shared ... a blessing received.

Footnotes:

[1] *Daily Texts* 2013, © 2013 by Mount Carmel Ministries, 800 Mount Carmel Drive NE, PO Box 579, Alexandria, MN 56038. 320-846-2744. *www.MountCarmelMinistries.com* .

[2] Dr. Gary Smalley is a family counselor, president and founder of the Smalley Relationship Center and author of books on marriage and family relationships from a Christian perspective.

Favorites

"So, if you think you are standing firm, be careful that you don't fall! No temptation has seized you except what is common to man. And God is faithful; he will not let you be tempted beyond what you can bear. But when you are tempted, he will also provide a way out so that you can stand up under it."
1 Corinthians 10:12-13

The dogwoods and redbuds nestled against the Smoky Mountains would be at their peak. Springtime in the Smokies is worth a special trip.

Lacey, too, was excited about the flight to east Tennessee. The plane couldn't get off the Houston tarmac fast enough for her. But it wasn't thoughts of dogwoods or redbuds that caused the glow. No, the week ahead meant she and Charlie would be together. It meant being on his arm at his senior prom.

She was in a bubbly mood! They had met at a Texas panhandle church camp two years ago when youth from around the country had gathered. And a Tennessee/Texas romance blossomed. The home-made bracelet around her wrist was testimony. The alternating beads of red ("his favorite color") and orange ("Tennessee orange, of course") embraced his name, Charlie ("my favorite guy!"). The companion bracelet she held, of lime and blue beads ("my favorite colors!") and anchoring her name, would be her special gift to him at the airport.

Lacey is 16, the youngest of three daughters. "I'm the baby. My oldest sister is 22; she was born in North Dakota. My middle sister is 19, and we were born in Texas."

She was 8 when her parents divorced. "Yeah, they fought a lot. There was always a lot of yelling in the house, but that was normal. So, I was scared when it happened. My sisters finally explained the divorce to me. It's just what happens, they said, when two people don't get along."

Her dad grew up in Wisconsin and is an Air Force veteran. He works for a large defense contractor. "He used to do nose art on airplanes, but now writes technical manuals. Mom was a military brat growing up, and today works in a doctor's office."

The family was devout in the Baptist tradition. "I was in church on the first Sunday of my life, and I never miss. Neither of my parents have remarried, and even after the divorce we still went to church every Sunday."

To stay in the same school district, she moved in with her grandma and lived with her for a few years. "Dad moved back into the district a couple years ago, so I've lived with him since. I've always had a good relationship with him. He had a girlfriend for a while but it didn't work out. He's looking for the right lady, but he has certain standards. He wants a Godly woman."

What about Mom?

"Mom has a boyfriend now, and I went to lunch with him last weekend."

And your sisters? Do you see each other?

"My oldest sister started seeing a bunch of guys and got pregnant at 16. She dropped out of school in tenth grade, had a son, and started seeing another guy who got her involved with drugs and alcohol, and tattoos. I pretty much raised my nephew, along with my mom and my other sister. Eventually my sister regained custody, and then she got pregnant again. So now I have a niece, too. They live in Oklahoma. She's gotten married and has started going back to church.

"I'm not going to make my life like that. I was close to her when I was small. But my middle sister will not forgive her for the messes she made of her life and ours. The good news is, the guy she married has two other kids, and they've both straightened out their lives.

"My middle sister has been married for nine months to a Navy guy. She's not church-centered, though. She thinks life is all about her.

"Dad is close to the oldest sister, not so much with the second one. Mom isn't in good relations with my oldest sister, but she does get along well with my middle sister."

It was time to take the conversation in a different direction. "What gives you joy, Lacey? What are the things that make you laugh?"

Any activity that centers on Charlie is a favorite. "We love to Skype!" She glowed as she talked of him. "Charlie is my first serious boyfriend."

What's ahead for Charlie? "Well, he will go to college. But I'm not sure what he wants to do. I'm not sure he knows yet, either. He likes cars, likes to detail them, and he likes messing with engines. Or maybe he'll be a gym teacher, because he likes sports, especially soccer and football. And he's crazy about Tennessee football!"

What about you? Is it Texas or Tennessee? "Oh, no question. Texas is the best!" She likes George Bush, but not President Obama.

"How can you like George Bush? He's Methodist!" I exclaimed. "But he's Texan!!" she was quick in reply as the laughter flowed.

We returned to sources of joy and happiness. "I like hanging out with my best friend, doing girly stuff. Getting pampered. Tomorrow I'm getting my nails done."

Church continues to be at the center of her life. "A few weeks ago, we had a babe-bash. It was an overnight at the church just for girls. The juniors and seniors served dinner to the underclassmen. We had sessions on fashion, on how relations honor God, on self-worth. We worshipped, and broke into small groups by grade for prayer time. It was an accountability night, where we shared about life content. We do this once a year, and usually about thirty girls come. It's powerful."

She's been attending this church for about three years. "The church where I was born and raised has kind of gone downhill, so it's nice to be a part of a growing, vibrant church. The high school group has about sixty kids and it's a lot of fun."

Lacy likes sports too, especially basketball. She was recently part of *Upward*, a Christian-based basketball program. "It was fun and very competitive."

On the more serious side, she enjoys math and art. "I'm thinking of maybe teaching, or maybe interior design."

Lacey was a remarkable young woman who, at 16, was so at ease expressing her thoughts. Yes, teen giggles sprinkled the conversation. Even so, my curiosity led me to the query.

"Lacey," I began, "you know the card I gave you with my name and *the Query*, on it? Let's turn to that. Remember that I described a book I've been reading, that it's a collection of writings by several authors? And that one of them wrote the phrase that has become the query: *Always be prepared to answer the question when somebody asks, of the reason for the hope that is within you … and do so with gentleness and respect.*

"So, Lacey – *what is the reason for the hope that is within you?*"

"Yes, I remember," she said softly. She sat quietly for a few moments with her eyes on her lap. "I think …" and there followed a long pause. She turned to me, and continued slowly, "I think I don't really know what it means exactly, because I have a young mind, still …". Her countenance was serious. There was no teen giggling. She was deep in thought, searching.

"Well," I continued. "Maybe it would help you to know that the book I'm talking about is the Bible. And this author was Peter, and it comes from 1st Peter in chapter 3, verse 15. Does that help?"

She had earlier seen my travel Bible, and asked if she could borrow it. Perhaps no surprise, she found the text quickly. She studied it for several minutes.

"Nobody has ever asked me that before," she began. "But now that I know where it comes from, I think I can answer it. *What is the reason for my hope?* I guess it's because I know that God is always going to be there, and in the end, I am going to have eternal life with Him. And He put me here for a reason, to be a light for Him and to help others."

I was struck by her response. She was looking at me with a quiet confidence. She wasn't looking for affirmation of her answer. It was simply a look of quiet certainty.

"Would you like to know my favorite Bible verse?" she asked.

She leafed to 1st Corinthians, and read the verses aloud softly:

> *"So, if you think you are standing firm, be careful that you don't fall! No temptation has seized you except what is common to man. And God is faithful; he will not let you be tempted beyond what you can bear. But when you are tempted, he will also provide a way out so that you can stand up under it."*

She shared that she referred to these verses on Facebook for some friends who were struggling, and they have since told her that the verses helped them. "I have seen people come closer to God because of these verses."

What makes them *your* favorite?

"It helps me to know that God always provides ways out when you're tempted," answered Lacey. "That God will never fail you. That He is always there, always close. That He is the only one who can save you and will truly love you, with unconditional love."

As she bounded into Charlie's arms past security, young love was in the air. Giggles. Hugs. The blue and lime bracelet gifted, and the red and Tennessee orange one admired. More giggles. Walking past them, I couldn't help but giggle, too.

A story shared ... a blessing received.

Unresolved

*"How could a person with one breath be in a state of euphoria, suffering delusions
of grandeur and believing herself to be in possession of Ultimate Truth
with the power to foretell the future, and with the next be plunged
into the foul-tasting waters of deepest depression?"*
Helen Moeller, from *Tornado*[1]

She was returning to her East Coast home after a couple weeks in California. She, too, was grateful for the extra room of an empty middle seat during the four-hour flight ahead. Conversation unfolded easily. She was about my age, friendly and mature, and expressed her thoughts clearly. Stylish, streaked hair complemented a trim figure.

In time, out came *The Query* card. Curiosity crossed her face as she studied it. "Well, Larry," she smiled, "I'm Sharon. Ok, we have plenty of time. I'm game, but I'm not sure there's much to learn."

She grew up on a small farm in the Northwest with her parents and an older brother, and saw a lot of hardship at an early age. "It was a general-purpose farm. We raised grain and animals to sustain ourselves."

Both parents were alcoholics. "Dad was very abusive when he drank, and very good when he didn't."

Elementary school was in a country two-room schoolhouse with first through fourth grades on one side, and fifth through eighth on the other. The closest town (population, 3,000) was 8 miles from the farm, so riding the bus was a part of growing up. High school was small, with a senior class of forty-two.

Her dad learned automotive repair at a trade school, and mom was a telephone operator at the phone company. "We had a party line growing up," she chuckled as she recalled some party line experiences.

"Dad was very involved in the Catholic religion. When they married, Mom converted to it. So, my brother and I were raised in the church. For my first 4 years, I attended a Catholic school. And I was confirmed in the church."

Sharon attended a Catholic nursing school and married in the church at 24. "My husband was raised Lutheran. When we married, he switched to Catholic. But we weren't very steadfast," and they found themselves drifting from church. Eventually, they divorced.

She learned that she was unable to have children. "And then I met Nate. Nate had been married, and had four children. So, having more children wasn't important to him." They married, but since she and Nate were both divorcees they weren't able to marry in the Catholic church. The oldest son, Ben, is 35 and struggles with bi-polar and addiction. He lives in the west with his mother. His mom is also bi-polar, and borderline schizophrenic. The younger son dabbled in drugs for years, but has been clean for the last 5.

The dysfunction in the family took its toll, and divorce followed. After being apart for 4 years, she and Nate remarried and altogether have been married for 24 years.

"Nate has been very successful in business," she continued. "Today, he owns a company based in India and he lives there 9 months of the year. He comes back to the U.S. three times a year, and I visit there about three times a year, too." But she has no desire to live in India.

Sharon seems resigned to the situation, and has found purpose working part-time at a hospital near her home. She was relieved to learn of the thread of bi-polar and addiction in my family fabric, too. And that brought us to the query.

"So, Sharon," I posed, after a few moments of quiet, *"what is the reason for the hope that is within you?"*

She looked at me intently. "I guess my hope was from the strength and resilience that I learned as a child. I tried things, and when I succeeded, those successes gave me strength to know I could be what I would be. Maybe what gives you hope is that you can see good, even amidst the bad."

Our conversation returned to faith and the church. Sharon re-engaged in the church 15 years ago after the restart of her second marriage, but not in the Catholic tradition. She, instead, goes to a Methodist church. Her church has lots of groups and activities, including a homeless ministry and a ministry to shut-ins. "I guess I can identify with the people there."

"How has returning to church influenced me?" she asked, repeating my question. "I guess it has given me an inner strength. I talk to God all the time. That is just a part of my life. I've been very pleased with my life and am thankful for it, and I attribute that to God in my life."

She attended Rick Warren's church in southern California for several years before moving to the East Coast. "I confess to having had some trepidation about going back to the Catholic church after being estranged from it. And I guess the reality that they wouldn't recognize my remarriage didn't help."

While Sharon is a 'regular' at a Methodist church, her private prayer life often includes prayers to Mary and the saints, a practice from which she takes much comfort. "I stopped praying the rosary years ago, but praying to Mary remains an important part of me."

The announcement to return tray tables and seats to upright positions signaled the end of note-taking, but the conversation continued earnestly. We went deeper into the shared experiences of strained relations with adult children complicated by addiction, bi-polar, and schizophrenia and the difficulty of navigating 'tough love'. To love, but not to enable.

Sharon's mood turned somber as we neared the gate.

"Thank you, Larry," she said softly. "This conversation has made me realize that there are some unresolved issues between me and Ben. And we've got to work them out, as hard as that may be. I know I need to do that, to have peace."

A story shared ... a blessing received.

[Author's note: It was a delight to receive this beautiful handwritten note from 'Sharon' within weeks of mailing her the initial draft.]

Dear Larry,

I have finished reading The Query on Sunday afternoon. As I read the life stories, I felt thankful, encouraged and sometimes saddened and reflective.

You told my story well, and I am pleased with your accounting.

Thank you for sharing my story.

'Sharon'

Footnote:

[1] *Tornado: My Experience with Mental Illness*, by Helen Moeller © 1967 by Fleming H. Revell Company, PO Box 6287, Grand Rapids MI 49516 (616) 676-9185   Library of Congress Catalog Card Number 68-11366.

Principled Living

"Happy are those who find wisdom, and those who get understanding, for her income is better than silver, and her revenue better than gold."
Proverbs 3:13-14 (NRSV)

He was among the last to board, so it was no surprise that he settled into the aisle seat. This Chicago flight to California connected through Denver, and at least for that leg we would enjoy an empty middle seat. He smiled as we exchanged greetings. His distinctive accent put to rest whether there might be a Query on this flight. He was in his twenties, clean cut and athletic, professional in appearance.

As we reached cruising altitude, I extended my hand and my card. "My name's Larry. Are you heading home, or going visiting?"

He shook my hand, studied my card, smiled and said "Hi! I'm Rabur. I'm going home."

"Well hello, Robert," I smiled back. "Nice to meet you."

"No," he clarified politely. "It's Rabur. Not Robert. Rah'-ber, spelled R-a-b-u-r. It's Polish. There's no 't' at the end."

He was curious about *'the Query - a book project'*. After reflecting on the nature of the project, his story began to unfold.

Rabur was born in Poland and came to the United States at 17 to join his dad in New York City. His mom remains in Poland with a younger brother. A sister (an artist) and two brothers live in New York.

After staying with his dad for a while, he struck out for Texas and worked in the oil fields building oil rigs. Eventually he returned to New York, entered City University of New York and in 2008 received a degree in chemical engineering. Upon graduating, he joined a Fortune 500 company as a process engineer. Today he works in a 100-employee plant manufacturing various grades of industrial additives. He aspires to more responsibility in operations management, preferring that to engineering or technology. He rents a house, not an apartment.

The conversation turned to outside interests. He enjoys reading, and is about halfway through *The Magic of Thinking Success*, by David Schwartz. Why that book? "I enjoy stretching myself."

Rabur was born in 1982, raised on a farm in Poland, and enjoyed boyhood there. At about age nine, his family moved near a large city to a suburb of 60,000 population. He is the second of five children: Oskar (age 31), a store manager in Yonkers; Rabur (29); Igor (23), with the NYPD; Nadia (22), a hairdresser and struggling artist; and Xajak (16), living in Poland with Mom.

"Mom and Dad have been living apart for about ten years. Mom came to New York and stayed for 6 months, then returned to Poland where she teaches in a neighborhood school." Do you see your mom often? "Not really. I've been back to Poland twice in the last 11 years."

What was it like, growing up? "It was a general farm, about fifty acres. Mom was teaching, and Dad was in construction. It was four kilometers to school from the farm, and we walked. Grandma tended the farm, and there were chores to do, cows to milk. But eventually the farm was sold. Dad was building his own house in the suburb, and he traveled a lot back and forth while building the house. Mom still teaches, even though she is retired."

As Rabur was relating his story, I wondered whether he remembered the solidarity movement in Poland. So, "Hmmm. If you were born in 1982, do you remember the Solidarity movement in Poland? What was it like?"

"Oh yes, I remember," he smiled. "In the 1980's as communism was winding down, there were no toys, no candy, no TV, no clothing, no shoes. The government dictated one pair of shoes a year for each child. By the 1990's, we were living in the suburbs in the three-story home Dad had built, with six bedrooms. When communism ended, suddenly everything became available. Cars, cell phones. In my mind, the transformation was overnight. In 1990, you could go to the store and get as much as you wanted of what you wanted. The change was very welcome!"

At the onset of the free market in 1990 his dad went to New York, having heard of more opportunity in the United States. "Dad was able to get a passport, so off he went to New York. He was there for 2 years, while we were all still in Poland. He came back and finished building the house and began exploring a side business, buying and selling cars. Dad would travel to western Europe, pick up some cars, and bring them back to Poland to sell."

What drew your dad to the U.S.?

"Dad's great grandfather – my great, great grandfather – emigrated to the U.S. in the 1800's. His son, my dad's grandpa, was born in the U.S. somewhere in Pennsylvania or West Virginia and they were coal miners. So, they were a Polish family living in the U.S.!

"When great, great grandpa was ready to retire, the family moved back to Poland. My grandma was born in 1918 in Poland to my American-born great grandfather. Because she was born to an American citizen, she had citizenship rights in America. For Dad, then, it was much easier to get a green card. In 1990 he moved to the U.S. to make more money. He stayed for 2 years and did well in construction and earned about $120/day. In Poland, the same labor would have brought about $10/day.

"After 2 years, he had enough wealth to come back to Poland. With the money he had made, he finished building the house in the suburbs, and with freedom growing in Poland it was easy to go back and forth. So he worked construction in both countries. But he grew tired of being on the road all that time, so Mom and Dad moved to the U.S. We stayed behind in Poland with Grandma."

And Grandpa?

"I never knew Grandpa. He died in the 1950's right after Dad was born.

"Dad stayed in the U.S. while Mom returned to her teaching job by the end of that summer. Between school terms, she would go back to the U.S. for a couple months at a time. It meant a lot of travel and a lot of disruption. The 90's were hard on the family."

In Poland, teaching is very respected so his mom was committed to keeping her job. "Dad could have had a normal job and a normal life with Mom, but he desired an improved life style and a higher standard of living."

Rabur was the first child to go to the U.S. after finishing high school. "I was the first to get a high school degree, because my older brother had taken the 'trades' track which meant it took him three years longer." In Poland, after high school a single man either trained for the military (if physically fit) or traveled. So, with two options, Army or travel, he set out to visit his dad in New York.

"Because Dad had extended family in America from past generations, they were excited about my coming. I lived with him in New York for about ten years. In 2001, two of my brothers followed, and eventually my sister. So, our youngest brother is still in Poland with Mom."

What was it like, growing up?

"In Poland the legal drinking age is 18. As teens, we would go dancing in clubs. Even though our town was small, there were almost 2,000 kids in school, and everybody knew everybody." He stays in touch by e-mail and Facebook.

What about romance? Is there someone special?

"I'm available!" he laughed.

Last year, his company transferred him to the West Coast. He's disappointed with the lack of variety in cultural activities or things to do. "It's not New York," he noted. He finds it hard to meet people, to experience different mindsets. "Where I live now, most people seem very settled and comfortable in their communities. In New York, everybody is an outsider so the city is much more diverse. I miss that. It's been a culture shock, moving from New York City to the west."

Rabur likes his job. "As a process engineer, I help keep the lines running smoothly and I'm always working to improve the way we do things. The additives we make are used in a lot of products that touch peoples' lives and helps to improve them. I like that. And getting to the bottom of a problem to keep a line up is rewarding. I know that if a line goes down, it can mean folks being sent home until it comes back up and that means a short paycheck which affects their families. So, it's very satisfying. But the 24/7 'on call' can get a little demanding. I can handle the fifty-to-sixty hours a week, but the calls in the middle of the night get old."

What about time away from work? Any hobbies?

"Anything outdoors," he grinned. "I love snowboarding, and travel. Traveling around the U.S., and now exploring California. Sightseeing. Hiking. Camping. And I do like the diversity of San Francisco, even though it's smaller than New York. So, I enjoy visiting there with friends and going out to dinner."

Conversation shifted as Rabur asked about my life experiences. He was fascinated by the concept of executive search, of helping companies find top-flight people for demanding jobs. He wanted to know about Alaska, about growing up on a farm in the Midwest, about how *The Query* project had begun, and of some of the stories I'd gathered.

It was time for the query.

"So, Rabur, *what is the reason for the hope that is within you?*"

He was thoughtful for a bit. His responses were slow, measured.

"I like helping people. I like making a difference. I like knowing that what I do affects other people. I like to be part of something new, part of progress. I like to think. And I like to see the fruit of my hard work.

"It's all part of a big circle."

I shared that I was moved that, at his relatively young age, he has a remarkable sense of how his little piece in a huge corporation fits into the big picture – of his sense that his work affects the lives of people around the world who rely on the products his company manufactures.

He smiled. "When I was in the university in New York, I worked in restaurants for 5 years. It was my job to make sure people enjoyed their evening, and I got paid for doing that! I guess my future will be about how I can touch more lives."

What's next, then? "I'm not sure. I'm thinking of moving to South America for a while just to see what that is like."

"What about faith, or church?" I asked. "Has that been a part of your life?"

He was born into and raised in the Catholic tradition. His parents often took them to church, and they celebrated all the holidays, "and I still celebrate them."

"But I don't go very often anymore. It's not because I don't have faith, but there are just too many other social influences. Too many churches get into political matters that shouldn't be a part of religion. So, I stopped going some years ago. I still go for holidays and when someone gets married, but church just isn't a regular habit for me."

And the last time you were in church? "A little over a year ago in New York. I was a groomsman in a friend's wedding. It made me start to think about church a little bit."

"But now that I think of it, not long ago I went to a Polish Catholic church. I'm hoping maybe that's a place where I can find a Polish community and learn about stores and food that I like. Those things are hard to find in a general supermarket. And, who knows, maybe I'll meet a girl!" My eyebrows rose, and we both laughed.

"I've never really thought about how the faith has shaped me. I'm sure it probably has. But I have my own opinion about things.

"The bishop who gave me confirmation later was dismissed for doing side things with gangs and the mafia. They were molesting new priests in Poland. And there was another priest that wasn't using the church's money the way it was intended. He was siphoning it off for his personal use. So, I guess I've become a cynic of the church. Not the faith, but the church."

He was quiet for a few moments, in thought.

Then he continued. "Some of the teachings are valuable for living. And so, why not take those parts which are useful and incorporate them into my life? The institutional church may not be helpful to me, but parts of the teaching are.

"I like to live by principles, not by the organized management system of the church."

Once again, I was struck by the earnestness of this young man. A young man who strives for principled living.

A story shared ... a blessing received.

[Author's note: Some weeks after mailing the initial draft, Rabur's brief handwritten note in reply reflected his personality.]

Hi Larry!

Thanks for capturing this (my) story. I was shocked by the title of the chapter (Principled Living); you nailed it!

Also, you captured the story beautifully; I don't have anything to add or delete.

Sorry it took me a while to get back to you, however I hope the book gets published and I'm looking forward to reading it.

'Rabur'

Everything Changed

"May the God of hope fill you with all joy and peace in believing, so that you may abound in hope by the power of the Holy Spirit."
Romans 15:13 (NAB)

Cradled in her lap was *Tender at the Bone*, a book by Ruth Reichl. "Enjoying the book?" the conversation began.

"Oh, it's okay," she replied. "I love to cook, love to feed my family, and it was in my mother-in-law's library so I thought it might be a fun read on a long flight. It's okay, if you like reading about cooking."

They were heading home to their small town in northeast Indiana. "We've been in Redding visiting my husband's father for a few days. He moved out there a few years ago. It's always nice to visit, but it's better to get home."

Having lived in northwest Ohio early in my career, conversation flowed easily about that part of the country. It wasn't long before introductions. She took my card, studied it, and said, "Hi, Larry. I'm Kris, and this is Todd."

In their early-fifties, they are a couple who seem to share a quiet enjoyment in the company of the other. Kris was fashionably dressed with auburn hair stylishly kept. She is a beautiful woman, with a warm, smiling face. Todd is ruggedly handsome with a masculine presence, enhanced by the well-trimmed moustache.

We all shook hands. "What does this mean, *The Query – a book project*?" Kris asked. "Are you looking at books?"

I explained *The Query* and asked whether she would be open to answering some questions while I made a few notes, to add her story to those gathered so far. They watched as I leafed quickly to the next empty page.

"Sure," she replied. "But you should be talking to Todd. He's better at those kinds of things."

"Well, Todd didn't sit beside me. So, you're the lucky one today." And then, leaning past her, "Are you ok with that, Todd?"

Todd grinned. "This will be fun! I'm going to enjoy listening."

I explained my interest in a book, a compilation of writings by several authors, and that one of them had included a phrase which intrigued me: *Always be prepared to give the answer to the question when someone asks, of the reason for the hope within you. And do so with gentleness and respect* …. And that, for some time, it has become my project to ask the question and listen to the stories.

"So, Kris, this is your lucky day. It's your turn. *What's the reason for the hope within you?* Sometimes it's helpful to me to listen to the life story, because it seems that somewhere along the way, the answer to the query comes out of the life story. So maybe it will be easier to just tell me a little of your life."

"Oh," Kris giggled. "That will be easy! I love to talk about my family."

She is a Hoosier, through and through. A native of that northeast Indiana town, her father was a plumbing contractor and her mom, a stay-at-home mom. They raised five children, so Kris has three sisters and a brother. She is the second oldest.

Todd grew up in the same area; he was her high school sweetheart. They have been married 33 years and have two grown children: a daughter, 28, getting a PhD in integrated bio-medical science and expecting a baby soon; and a son, 25, a brick mason. He lives nearby in the country, and has a fourteen-month old daughter, their only grandchild. Grandma Kris delights in watching her every moment she can.

Kris attended a technical school and worked part time in doctors' offices. Todd is a bankruptcy attorney. For many years, he was a solo practitioner, but 4 years ago joined a partnership.

My business curiosity kicked in. We were a couple years into the economic downturn with bankruptcy filings commonplace. "Todd," I leaned over, "there seems to be an awful lot of bankruptcies these days, and it seems that many of them are folks taking advantage of the system to walk away from their obligations. Has that been your experience?"

"No," Todd replied. "It's been my experience that our clients are generally fine, hardworking people who have been caught in some unfortunate situations. Most of them have resisted bankruptcy until it's been their only alternative. They're good people, just having some bad luck. It is satisfying to be able to help them work through a tough time."

His answer surprised and heartened me. Here, a kind-hearted bankruptcy attorney!

Back to Kris. "What gives you joy in life, Kris? What do you enjoy?"

"I love to entertain, and I enjoy exercise," she replied with a smile.

Her 74-year-old mom lives next door and about a year ago began to exhibit signs of dementia. More and more, Kris finds herself tending to her. "Dad was diagnosed last year with pancreatic cancer and died 9 months later. It was hard on Mom, and all of us."

How does the dementia manifest itself, with your mom?

"We're fortunate that she is still able to live in her home, but now she needs help paying bills. She needs to be reminded of things. Because she no longer can drive, it means driving her places and getting groceries. We're lucky that all five siblings live close by." Kris devotes about 2 hours a day with her, and knows that will grow. "It makes me sad. I'm the only one of the five who doesn't work, and since I live next door, much of it falls to me. But that's okay. Our family has always been close, which makes it a little easier."

Todd's father is a retired pharmacist. He's divorced and remarried, and moved to California.

"Okay, Kris. That family story is helpful. Now let's turn to the query. *What is the reason for the hope that is within you?*"

She thought for a moment. Her response came easily. "I'm a born again Christian. I know there's a heaven, and I know I'm going there. That's the reason for my hope.

"I'm at a very enjoyable time of life," she continued. "Each phase of life has been joyful: my kids, my family. I'm very much at peace and enjoying the aging process. It's been a great ride, even though there have been some bumps along the way."

What have been some of the bumps?

"I lost my brother-in-law 5 years ago at age 53 to lung cancer. He died within 3 weeks, and wasn't a smoker. And of course, my dad's death was tough. But neither he nor my dad were bitter at death. They, too, were confident of heaven in their future."

We sat for a bit in silence, and then continued. "Kris, if you're comfortable, I'd like to dig a little deeper. When I posed the query, you began by saying that you're a born-again Christian. Tell me about that."

"In 1997, we were attending a different church. I was raised in a church setting, but had never said the Prayer of Salvation. It was the day after Christmas. I was by myself and for some reason, it was that prayer that came to me and I prayed it. And everything changed."

Why? What prompted you to say that prayer, then, on that day?

"I don't know. I just had this yearning, this feeling that I wasn't quite right with God. Just a stirring within me. I just knew I had to say that prayer."

"And what is that prayer?" I asked.

"It's asking God to come into your heart. To change you, to live in you, to be in you. And everything changed at that moment. I can't explain it, but everything changed. It wasn't any great moment in church. No laying on of hands. Just a private moment when God came into my life. Everything changed. I was born again."

I was listening, not writing. So, I turned to my notebook and wrote. Again, we sat in silence. Then ...

"Tell me about your journey of faith ... your church life. What was it like?"

Kris was born and raised in a small Methodist church. They walked about a half-mile down the road. At some point, three small country Methodist churches merged into one. She and Todd were married in that church.

When first married, they drifted from church and didn't attend very regularly. A nurse in the doctor's office where she was working was married to a minister. "We got to know her and her husband and began visiting their church. They were Presbyterian." They liked his style of preaching and ministry, "and we raised the kids there."

But the pastor died suddenly of a heart attack. Things changed in the church, and they drifted away again. Later, after the life-changing prayer and God in her life, they joined a Friends (i.e., Quaker) church.

What led you to the Friends church?

"We were looking around, and were drawn to the modern worship, to the music style, to the messages. Today we attend regularly but are not immersed in the activities. There's been a change in pastors, so things are a little different now. And with the demands at home with Mom, I'm not able to volunteer very much."

How has church shaped your answer to the query?

"My life is very faith based," she noted, "with the certainty of heaven, and a place for me there. As a believer, as a follower of Jesus, I try to be a good person. I try to lead a life He would want me to live. I go to church to worship and honor Him. Not out of obligation, but because I want to."

"Kris, I'm not intimately familiar with the Friends church, but my perception is that it would lean more to the orthodox or conservative side of the Christian family. For someone raised Methodist, and then a while in the Presbyterian church, what has it been like to transition to Friends?"

"Oh, yes," she smiled. "Ours is a very strict church, and I love the people there. But I don't necessarily follow everything they believe in, but you can say that about anybody in any church. There are things I question, but I still know I'm on the right path."

I closed the notebook. Session over.

I leaned over to Todd. "Well, Todd, what was it like to eavesdrop on that conversation?"

"I enjoyed it," he smiled. "I learned a little more about my wife, and why I love her. It made me think about some of the questions you were asking – and I've been reflecting that we don't take the time to listen to people anymore. I'm glad I was one seat away, so I could just listen."

With a smile on her face, Kris noted, "I still think you should have talked with Todd. He's the philosopher of the family!"

And we parted, bidding Godspeed to our travels.

A story shared … a blessing received.

[Note from the author: After their review of *Everything Changed* in the draft manuscript, Todd's handwritten letter was warm and gracious, with these excerpts.]

Dear Larry,

The draft of *The Query* is a very interesting read. This came at a very difficult time, but it was at the right moment. Kris' mother's dementia had entered into its final phases and she just passed away last week. It has been an arduous process. Reading this effort gave me a boost when I needed it, and so it reshaped my attitude and approach in trying to assist Kris and her family in dealing with all of it.

Since we met, we have continued to be blessed. We now have five grandchildren and continue to enjoy this phase of our journey. We also have been subjected to many trials, but perhaps those are for another chapter. Despite all the troubles, we still would respond to your query in the same fashion and with an even greater hope.

Todd & Kris

Balance

> *"First there is the fall, and then we recover from the fall.*
> *Both are the mercy of God."*
> Julian of Norwich

I'm not so sure what I think about the above statement, to be honest.

I'm not so sure how to view any fall as the mercy of God.

I was reflecting earlier in an email to a dear friend of mine that there are times that God surprises me.

In fact, God surprises me almost as much as God disappoints me. I wish I could say it were the other way around, but perhaps my fatalistic purview clouds my vision. Or rather experience over purview.

In any event, I like the above quote. It challenges my oft deistic theology, one that is constantly in flux anyway. For as much as my life's experiences leave me wanting when it comes to God's presence, I have a high hope that there is an activity that goes on unbeknownst by me.

I do not need to know, I suppose. I just need to trust. For today, as with any other day, I see in a mirror dimly. And that is probably better than seeing fully.

A blog post, by Colleen E.M. Maillie[1]

The flight through Denver would afford ample time for homework ahead of the meeting later that day in Omaha. There were reports and grant applications stuffed in the seat pocket and stacked on the fold-down tray. There would be no time for *The Query* on this leg.

The 'Hello!' was polite but lacked energy; his eyes, heavy. He was clean cut with a muscular Kiefer Sutherland build and was wearing a black baseball cap, black t-shirt, and jeans. Occasionally, he glanced at the reports on my tray as one followed the other.

An hour into the flight, it was time for a study break. He had caught some catnaps along the way and now seemed fully alert.

"So, are you a Cornhusker?"

"No, not really," he replied.

Where's home? "Lincoln."

Lincoln, and not a Cornhusker. How can you live in Lincoln and not be a Cornhusker?

"It's just not that important to me. I appreciate that it is important to many in Nebraska, and it gives them something to talk about and get excited, but I guess I just don't get as caught up in it."

So, you're heading home on a Tuesday morning. What took you to Denver? Passing through?

"Yeah, passing through. I zipped over to San Francisco Saturday to take in the 49ers game last night."

Ah, that's why he'd been nodding off. Recovery from football frenzy. "Yeah, it was fun," he grinned. "I'm just getting a little balance in my life. "

The phrase intrigued me. A young man in his 30s, I'd guess, wearing a silver-colored wedding band.

"Tell me about that ... 'balance' in your life. What does that mean?"

He began sharing his philosophy of living – that it's important to have a balanced life. That too many people put emphasis in one aspect of their lives, while other parts suffer. "In fact, I make it a part of my 'coaching' with the team at work, encouraging everybody to tend to more than just their work. That the outside-the-job part of their life needs balance, too."

What do you do, when you're not heading off to 49ers games?

"I'm vice president of sales for an equipment dealer/distributor in Lincoln and have a sales force of twelve reporting to me. So, I keep reminding them to keep their family and home life in balance with their job.

"Tell me," he asked, "why are you headed to Omaha?"

I described my role as a board member of a national men's ministry nonprofit, and that I was heading there for a two-day meeting of its fundraising committee to plan for the coming year.

"I couldn't help but notice that your reading material has 'Lutheran' across the top," he noted. "Are you a Lutheran?"

"Yeah, though I consider myself more a Christian and just happen to be a part of the Lutheran tribe. Are you familiar with any of that?"

"Oh, I guess I'm not into religion or churches," he said. "Seems to me that churches are just people who are critical of everybody who isn't part of their church. Pretty hypocritical, actually. Baptists don't seem to like Presbyterians; Presbyterians don't like Methodists; Methodists don't like Lutherans; and none of them seem to like Catholics. They all just seem to take potshots at each other. That's not the kind of religion I want to be a part of. Too much judging each other. Not a healthy place for me."

I let that set for a bit, pondering what he had said. He wasn't being disrespectful or condescending but, rather, simply sharing his observations. It wasn't an argumentative tone. Even so, I didn't want to go there.

A change in direction was needed. "So, what does it mean for you, this 'balance' in your life? What does your life look like? I see you wear a wedding ring. Is there a family?"

"Yes, I'm married with three kids: a 5-year-old daughter, a 3-year-old son, and a baby girl. She's two-and-a-half-months," he beamed. "For me, balance is being sure to put my wife and family at least equal to my job if not before. And it's important to carve out a little time for me, too. I like sports – always have. I played baseball all through school and still play on a team for recreation. I'm 39, and I'm the oldest guy on my team – and I do a pretty good job of keeping up with the young ones!" he chortled.

"Yeah, well, you'll outgrow that," my experience kicked in. "Your 39-year-old body isn't going to put up with that for much longer."

He laughed. "Oh, yeah! I'm a little stiffer in the mornings than I used to be. As long as I can, I'll stick with it. It's an important part of that balance in life."

So how did you scoot off to San Francisco all alone, and why the 49ers and not the Cornhuskers?

"Oh, I don't do that very often. I grew up in California, and the 49ers have been fun to follow through the years. So, it was a quick trip, part of that 'balance' thing."

The conversation was becoming a dilemma. We were only about a half-hour from touchdown in Omaha, and the conversation had taken an unexpected turn. *The Query* was not intended to be a part of this flight. I wanted to simply be a normal, detached passenger for a change – but it seemed like the conversation was taking us there.

I reached under the seat ahead and retrieved the notebook from my backpack. He watched as I opened it and took out a card and gave it to him. He studied it quizzically.

"You have a refreshing outlook on living," I continued. "For the last couple years or so, I've been gathering stories from folks, often on long flights with the person sitting next to me. I'm sure the stories will become a book – thus, the card. I hadn't intended to gather a story today, but yours is intriguing. So, in the time left, would you mind if I make some notes?"

He seemed hesitant.

"Your story will join quite a few others, as you can see." He watched intently as I leafed slowly through earlier entries in the becoming-tattered Moleskine©. Now he was intrigued.

"You do this often?"

"Well, I wouldn't say 'often'. I keep the notebook in the backpack, which goes with me everywhere. When I have an hour or so of empty time, that seems to be when the notebook comes out. Often on airplanes, but sometimes in a restaurant over a lunch hour, or in the customer lounge at a car dealer during a tune up, or once as part of a jury pool waiting to be called. Whenever I sit down with someone who seems to have a different life journey, I'll bring out the card. It's been quite the experience."

"How in the world did you ever get started on something like this?"

And so, I turned to the first entry. He watched and listened as I flipped through the pages and related the story of Quentin.

"Oh, by the way – as the card says, my name is Larry," I smiled, extending my hand. "Ahhh," he returned the smile, taking my hand. "I'm Cliff."

"Ok, Cliff. Nice to meet you."

"So, what's *The Query*?" he asked.

"Well, normally I come to the query after getting to know a little more about the person's life journey. But since we're already part way down that road, I guess we can turn to it first. Do you mind if I make some notes while we go? My memory ain't what it used to be," I smiled.

"No problem," Cliff laughed. It had helped that he had seen the pages of scribbles. I gathered his full name and contact information and his business card.

Because we had already touched a bit on church things, I explained my struggle with 1 Peter 3:15 and the experience on the Alaska flight leading to Quentin's story, which led to the query.

"So, Cliff, *what is the reason for the hope that is within you?*"

He turned thoughtful. "As a kid, you don't get it," he began. He talked of a focus on the immediate needs: food, clothes, a house. "In older years, you see the miracles of life happening daily. Overcoming tragedies. Helping each other. Hope is something like – well, like when you realize that there is more there than what is right in front of you."

He talked of his three young children and his wife, their stay-at-home mom. "We decided that was more important than a boat and a three-car garage."

She was raised Roman Catholic. His brother is a devout Lutheran. "What about you?" I asked. "How does faith shape your hope?"

"I'm an agnostic," Cliff replied, and then sat quietly for a few moments before continuing. "It's just that there is something beyond what we can see, an energy we're driven to."

I asked him to fill that in a little for me. He paused and stared out the window over the passing Nebraska farmland, thinking. "What drives us? Ego, I suppose. Greed. The negatives that come from the desire to want material things. All driving people in a bad way."

What about the agnostic part? What does that mean to you?

As an agnostic, Cliff believes there is a higher power, maybe even a God. "But no one knows the *real* truth," he said. "No one knows the whole story. It's our human need to want the complete answer – but there is so much unknown, so much recorded that isn't based on fact. Ok, Jesus lived, and Mohammed lived. It seems that everybody is scared to not have *the* answer - but without *an* answer, it's just chaos. So, religion provides *some* answers, some order, so that chaos is prevented."

He became silent, deep in thought. Reflective.

What about church, today? "No, the family isn't active in a church. I just don't see the need for it."

So, was faith or religion part of your growing up years?

"My dad wasn't religious at all. Mom was a Christian, but a hypocritical one. We never went to church. I guess, as a kid, I was an atheist. We just didn't do church."

The story unfolded further. His dad was a WW II veteran who was deeply affected by the war and plagued by alcoholism afterward. "We moved around a lot. Mom and Dad split when I was 8. So, I lived with my mom after that, and sort of lost touch with Dad. Dad died a few years ago; he was 77.

"Mom hooked up with an aircraft technician and it just seemed we kept moving, following wherever the aerospace industry took him, eventually ending up in Long Beach. When I turned 15, my mom and her cousin decided to ship me off to ranch life in Colorado, so I lived on my uncle's ranch through high school. It was good for me, living with my cousin. I learned how to pull a foal, castrate calves. I enjoyed it."

After high school, he jumped from college to college in Colorado and Nebraska and ended up earning a degree later in life. He married, but it ended after a couple years; "fortunately, with no kids," he sighed.

"One night, I went to meet a buddy at a bar and met a girl. She was nice. It just happened. And here we are, married going on eleven years and a great family."

He joined the distribution company after working for a supplier. A few years later, he was named head of sales.

Cliff takes pride in his team and that the business has grown almost fifty percent since he stepped into the sales management role. "I wear a shirt and tie every day, and so do all our reps. It's an important way to convey professionalism compared to our competitors."

The announcement signaling the final approach to Eppley Field brought *The Query* to a close. The last 30 minutes had been fascinating.

A story shared ... a blessing received.

Footnote:

[1] On her blog, *Pondering Heart*, by Colleen E.M. Maillie. *'20/20'* November 7, 2012. Searching and Servitude, on the WordPress.com weblog – http://ponderingheart.wordpress.com/2012/11/07/2020/. Used with permission.

Physics + Astrology

"Any job worth doing is worth doing perfectly."
Eddie Fisher[1]

"People hold a stereotype that you must be smart to be a nuclear physicist. You don't need any of that. You just have to be hard working," he said with conviction.

The Oak Ridge National Laboratory in east Tennessee is home to thousands of workers, including nuclear physicists. The regional commuter would funnel us through Chicago as our westward journey began. Nate would be attending a several-day conference in San Diego. He was an 'invited presenter', having been asked to share his experience with a unique apparatus designed and built to expand human understanding of nuclear structure. He would demonstrate the equipment in one session, and then conduct an experiment in another. Renowned physicists from around the world would be watching.

"No, I'm not nervous about the experiment or demonstrating the equipment. But I suppose when I'm standing in front of a couple hundred scientists who know a lot more than me … well, yeah, it'll probably take a few minutes to get past the butterflies," he grinned, a boyish grin. He seemed very young to be an 'invited' expert in the field of nuclear physics.

If the stereotype of a nuclear physicist means studious with wire-rimmed glasses, a wan appearance, thinning hair and nerdy demeanor – well, that's not Nate. He is a young man excited about living, not just nuclear physics. His eyes twinkled when he stretched out his hand to introduce himself, and settled into the aisle seat. "We're almost on top of each other in these little planes, so if I end up sitting next to some wacko, I want to know his name!" he grinned.

The chatter continued. Before long, *The Query* card appeared. Nate was intrigued. We compared notes on family, growing up, college, and career. The fascination with shared stories was mutual.

He grew up on a farm in the southeast, with two older sisters. "We had a couple cows, some chickens, a few goats and some sheep, and a dozen or so thoroughbreds. Cleaning pens and stables got old," he laughed. "No, I wasn't into 4-H. I did Boy Scouts instead."

Dad was a pharmacist, and Mom a registered nurse. "I was 16 when they divorced," he shared. His sisters were 18 and 23 then. "I'm 33 now," he acknowledged.

At 17, Nate left the farm and headed for college. Soon he was equipped with an undergraduate degree in physics, and not long after, a PhD. Three years of post-doctoral work found him at the Lawrence Berkeley National Laboratory in California. There, Beth came into his life. "We've been together 4 years. She came to Tennessee with me."

What is the reason for the hope within you?

He was quiet for a moment. "That can be broad and specific. What is the *source* of the reason for hope? Maybe that is the question.

"In some ways, Beth is the source of my reason for hope. We love each other, and we hope to get married."

His paternal grandparents were married for 60 years. His grandpa was in World War II. "They had faith in each other, faith in a relationship, faith in mankind. That seemed to be their reason for hope."

"Being taught you are capable is a source of hope. I had a physics advisor all through my coursework and early career, and we are still close. He instilled hard work in me. Karl would say, 'Take pride in what you're doing and do a good job. If you're not going to do a good job, then it's not worth doing.' Karl is my mentor, a model of success in my profession.

"I guess you could say that my career is my reason for hope. But that's a little different from why I like it. I like puzzles and games, and nuclear physics is a complex game. I hate being bored, and enjoy working hard.

"Nuclear physics can be a daunting task. It's like climbing a mountain. You don't focus on the peak when you're climbing. You focus on the next step. Nobody is born a mountain climber. Nobody is born a nuclear physicist. It's no different than playing a piano. I enjoy playing the piano, but few people are born good at the piano. It takes practice. With practice, you get good."

He spoke of the process of 'getting good' in nuclear physics. "It's no different than what you do. Whether in your work or in your book project, it takes staying with it. Practice. Focus on what is in front of you and the rest will follow. It's no different with nuclear physics."

After my note-taking caught up, we sat quietly for a few moments. I was curious about the influence of faith in his life, and whether faith has played a part in the reason for hope.

"My early childhood was Baptist, then about two-thirds of my upbringing was Episcopalian. But church isn't a part of my life, and it hasn't been for quite a while. I guess I'm religious, but not overly religious. I'm just not a big fan of organized religion.

"The church got too political and preachy about things that weren't relevant. But I still have a relationship with God, and it has a heavy impact on my conscious decision-making. So indirectly, I guess – yes, faith is a part of the reason for hope within me. Faith has an influence. I don't claim to understand why we're here. It just seems that there is a degree of expectation to be the best *you* you can be, which is not always so easy."

What about Beth? Is faith a part of her life?

"Beth is a stark contrast from how I was raised. She grew up in California. Her parents were raised Catholic, but they grew away from that and became affiliated with a Self-Realization Fellowship (SRF) led by yogis.

"Beth's mom is a nurse. Her mom grew up in Switzerland; her grandmother was French. Her dad is from Puerto Rico, so Beth is bilingual.

"Her parents became devoted astrologers, and so did Beth."

How does that work, in the relationship?

"In the beginning of our relationship, her belief and practice in astrology and my reluctance to entertain it caused many problems. I would always try to rationalize astrology, which usually just made Beth upset. Looking back on it, I can see that it was my arrogance getting in the way. In time, I admitted to myself and to her that science and logic can't explain everything. In fact, they aren't meant to. And even though I have no belief or faith in astrology, I have learned to listen with an open mind and withhold judgment or ridicule. Not surprisingly, there does seem to be a silver lining in this: Beth's sharing about astrology has prompted me to look at traits and flaws within myself and my piece in a relationship, which leads to awareness and self-improvement."

A thoughtful nuclear physicist, serious in relationship and excited about what lies ahead.

A story shared ... a blessing received.

[Note from the author – After receiving the initial draft of *The Query*, Nate's type-written letter in reply was gracious and affirming ... and characteristically thoughtful. Some excerpts --]

February 17, 2014

Dear Larry,

Thank you for sending me a copy of the manuscript *The Query*. I was pleasantly surprised to see my story included in the collection. I have read through many of the stories, including my own, and find them all very intriguing and revealing; stories such as these can't be fabricated, which highlights, in part, the true value of *The Query*.

Even now, I don't believe I'm prepared to answer w*hat is the reason for the hope within you?* At the time we met, I attempted to rephrase the question as "What is the *source* of the hope within you?" but I now realize that was my attempt to rationalize hope. However, hope seems to be an irrational quality of mankind that is arguably our greatest strength; without it, we're nothing more than machines. In essence, capacity for hope is what makes us human. I often feel hope with no rational source or reason. Why? I don't know. A higher power, a soul?

... ...
Sincerely yours,

(Nate)

---

[1] In 1966, Eddie Fisher was the meat department manager at Fareway Stores in Oelwein IA (my high school part-time job).

Broken Trust

*"O grant us help against the foe,
for human help is worthless."*
Psalm 60:11 (NRSV)

Small commuter jets may be efficient as regional connectors, but the 2x2 seating is a little too cozy when both seatmates are over 6 feet tall and carrying middle-aged spread. He had the aisle; I, the window. It would be a snug couple of hours.

He grinned as seat belts were unraveled and buckled in. As the runway receded, the conversation unfolded. It was one of those pleasant conversations, engaging but not intrusive. He was heading home after a few days in the Northwest; me, the last leg of a quick trip to the Midwest.

"What took you to that part of the country?" I asked.

"Oh, I had some personal things to take care of for a couple days," he replied. "So, what took you to Omaha?" he asked, almost in the same breath.

I'd attended a dinner the night before as part of a fundraiser for a national nonprofit. "It was hosted by Sapp Brothers Travel Centers," I shared. "Bill and Lee have big hearts and were gracious hosts. Are you familiar with Sapp Brothers? They're big across the Midwest. You see them along I-80 with water towers shaped like a campfire coffee pot."

"Oh, yeah," he nodded. "They're a good chain. I'm a long-haul truck driver, and when my load takes me in that part of the country, I stop at them. They're clean, and I like their stores. When I'm away for a while, it's a good place to pick things up for home."

"A long-haul truck driver? You mean, like, big rigs? Eighteen wheelers?"

"Yep, an eighteen-wheeler. I've been doing it for 20 years," he chuckled.

A company based in my recently-adopted Tennessee hometown had been embroiled in a controversy with trucking companies over a fuel rebate program, with regular stories in the local paper. "Oh yeah, I've heard about that. It's a small industry, and truckers like to talk – but I'm just a small operator, and most of my runs are along the west coast so it doesn't affect me."

A long-haul truck driver. What could be his reason for hope, I wondered?

Out came the card, the notebook, and the explanation of *The Query*.

"Sure, but I don't know what you're going to find interesting in the life of a truck driver." We shared a laugh.

Charlie has been an independent contractor for 20 years with his own rig. He operates solely for a large trucking company, and they pay him on a delivered-load basis. One of their dispatchers keeps him scheduled and watches for load sizes, which helps Charlie optimize his runs. "A good dispatcher makes you or breaks you in this business, and my guy has become like a good friend. He watches out for me and lets me decide which loads to accept. It's almost where I trust him with my livelihood, and that says a lot. I appreciate him."

He ran a garbage truck for 5 years before going out on his own; before that, he drove routes for a major beverage company.

He's 56 now. "My dad was Navy, and we moved a lot. I guess I was a Navy brat in the truest sense. My mom died in her early forties of stomach cancer; I don't remember much about her. I know I was 16 when she died, and I dropped out of high school. I have a brother who's a couple years younger than me. Dad remarried, and they were married 11 years before he died. A few years later, my stepmom died. So, it's me and my blood brother, and then we had two step-siblings: a teenaged brother in Mississippi, and a sister who died of a drug overdose a few years ago."

"I liked my dad, but we weren't real close."

At 30, Charlie got married. A year later, he earned his G.E.D. "I'd been driving either a delivery truck or a garbage truck and decided I wanted to do more, so it made sense to get my diploma." That marriage brought a daughter, Beth. It lasted 13 years. "We were worried about the public schools for Beth because of the terrible stories we'd heard, so we decided that Beth should be home schooled. I'd gotten into long haul trucking, and was sending money home. But with credit card after credit card, my wife's spending was way more than I made. And when she bought a new Mustang without telling me, that's when things fell apart. We got in so deep that bankruptcy was the only way out." The marriage ended soon after.

"It took a few years for me to re-establish a relationship with my daughter. It was rough, but we have a good one now. Beth's mom lives with her, which makes it tough. But her mom and I get along as well as we can."

The divorce court set alimony based on his gross earnings as a truck driver, rather than on the after-expenses net of a contractor. "Alimony was stiff. I kept it up, along with child support, until Beth turned 18 when child support was no longer required. I quit paying alimony then, too."

After a year of singleness, he met Donece at a NASCAR race in California. "We both like the races, and we've been together since. I don't know if we'll ever get married. It just doesn't seem important."

"Well, Charlie," I continued after catching up with the notes, "let's turn to the question: so, *what is the reason for the hope within you?*"

"I guess I have my grandpa to thank for that," Charlie observed. "'Never give up', he always said. 'Always strive forward. Make a plan and follow it.' I guess it was because of Grandpa that I always want to do good, to make something of myself. To be a provider. For me, it's about always doing the right thing, to have a peaceable existence."

His grandpa came from France, opened a garage and built a family business with a couple of gas stations, too. "That's the business my dad was born into and probably was where he learned the importance of respect.

"So while I have Grandpa to thank for this part of me, it seems like I get into trouble for always helping people out. Maybe helping them out more than them helping me."

His reflections turned to the marriage and his time on the road away from home, trying to make a decent living to support his wife and daughter. He fell silent. I finished jotting down his reasons for hope, set aside the pen, and reclined for a few minutes in the silence. Since there had been no mention of it, I gently broached whether faith or church had been a part of shaping his outlook.

"I have a hard time with religion," Charlie said quietly. "My grandparents and Dad always went to a Baptist church. I was baptized there. It seemed like we always had religion in the family. When we were young, my brother and I went to Sunday School all the time. I liked it.

"But when Dad got transferred out west, a lot changed. It was a tough adjustment for me. When I was 12, I got into trouble and ran away from home. The truancy police found me and took me to a detention center. There a Catholic priest talked with me. He told of a ranch where I could go and they would help me get through the tough times.

"That sounded a lot better than what I was doing, so I agreed. I thought it would be for a year, but when I arrived I learned it was a place for troubled juveniles who were there under court order, and that I would be there until I turned 18." He felt misled, betrayed, and scared. "But I couldn't get out because I had signed myself in and my dad had agreed."

Charlie stopped. So had my writing.

Slowly, his story continued to unfold. "One night after I'd been there a few weeks, the door to my room opened. The priest came in. He sat down on the bed beside me and began to rub my back. I didn't know what to do. I was only 12, and I didn't know what this was about. After a while, he left.

"That was just the beginning. I had heard some of the boys talk about 'night visits'. Some had laughed. Some cried. Most wouldn't talk about it.

"In time, the visits were about sex. Looking back on it now, I know that he 'had' me at least seventy times. But what could I do? What could anybody do? He said that we were there until we were 18, and that he had full say over our lives. We couldn't get out unless he signed the release documents.

"I wrote letters to my dad, letter after letter, telling him what was going on and begging him to get me out. But I never got an answer. I couldn't believe my dad wouldn't come and get me.

"Then late one night, when I was 14, I broke into the priest's office. I just had to call my dad, and the only telephone on the ranch was in that office. I called Dad's number, but the message said the number had been disconnected. It was the only number I had.

"I was scared, and knew I had to get out of the office and away from there. I saw some boxes, so I grabbed one, thinking I could stack them up to the window. The flaps weren't taped and as I carried the first one, I looked down. The boxes were filled with envelopes – envelopes containing letters that had never been mailed. Letters from other boys. My letters. Boxes of letters. I stacked them to the window as fast as I could, jumped, and ran. And ran and ran. I don't know how far it was to the highway, but I ran a long time.

"When I got to the highway, a trucker and his wife stopped and gave me a ride. I don't remember their names, but I remember that they took me over a hundred miles and helped me find my dad. He had moved, but they stayed with me until we found him.

"In the meantime, the priest had called Dad and told him that I had run away and that I would probably be trying to find him. The priest told him that those things happened sometimes, that the boys make up stories, and that Dad shouldn't worry because he would come to pick me up and take me back. "It's part of what the courts require us to do as overseers of the ranch," he told Dad.

"When I found my dad, the priest was already there, sitting at the end of the driveway in his car. I started to tell Dad everything, but he didn't believe me. When the priest came, and reached for my arm, I screamed – kicking and swinging my fists – because there was no way I was ever going back to that place. No way.

"Dad was shocked. He told the priest to leave and that we would work it out and he would bring me back to the ranch. I remember the priest telling Dad for my sake to 'keep it between us' so he wouldn't have to report it to the court and that way it wouldn't be on my public record. Finally, the priest left.

"I remember telling Dad everything from the beginning, but I don't know if Dad ever believed me. But at least he didn't take me back."

Charlie stopped. He seemed tired. After a bit, he continued.

"As the years went by, I just blocked all of that out of my memory. I guess that's how I coped with it.

"A couple months ago, 40 years later, I was at a truck stop. When I'm on break I often fire up the laptop to catch up on e-mail and stuff. That day, an article popped up about someone investigating past abuse of boys by a priest at a boys' ranch. When I saw the name of the place, I started shaking and broke into a cold sweat. There was the name of an attorney and a phone number.

"I couldn't sleep. I had written down the attorney information but didn't know what to do about it. Finally, I called him. He asked me a few questions over the phone and, after a short conversation, said he wanted to come and spend a day with me.

"A few weeks later, he did. He explained what he had learned, shared the names of some of the men who had told him their stories, guys I knew. He said that charges had been made against the priest, but that he had been reassigned by the diocese and then had died a few years ago. Now, claims were being filed against the diocese.

"He arranged for me to fly over and meet with a forensic psychiatrist. And that's where I've been for the last 3 days.

"I don't know what I'm going to say when I get home. Since that truck stop and as memories have come flooding back, I've shared some of it with my girlfriend, but not very much."

Charlie stopped. I could only listen. I couldn't write. He had shared unimaginable things.

He took a deep breath.

"You asked me about faith, about church. I know this: I will never go back to church. Never. The church ruined my life. The church knew something was wrong and covered it up. We now know that the diocese knew. They just moved him someplace else. Who knows who else was hurt? It was awful. Many of us were hurt, and we were just kids.

"Now I see why I struggled with things through the years, but I didn't understand. This is all new to me, the memories flooding back. It's awful. I put my trust in somebody and it was a terrible mistake. I have had a hard time trusting people, and now I know why."

We were both quiet as minutes passed. The plane was beginning its descent; we would land shortly.

I asked Charlie if he felt comfortable giving me his contact information so that I could get back in touch with him sometime. He did, and encouraged me to Google the ranch.

He turned away, and after a moment looked back at me. "I don't know why I shared all this with you. I don't know why. I'm almost sorry I did. It's a terrible story. Other than the psychiatrist, you're the only person I've told this much to. He told me that talking about it was something I would have to do, if I want to get past it."

He sat silently.

Then, "Maybe this is how I find healing. Maybe this is how I find peace. I don't know. But it just seemed to want to come out, and this time I decided to let it. I'm sorry that you were the one to hear it."

By the time I gathered my carry-on from the overhead, we were separated by several passengers. I watched him continue down the concourse as the distance grew between us. A solitary man immersed in his thoughts, reliving his past.

A story shared ... a blessing received.

Insights: *Listening*

Long bike rides are fun when the way is easy, Ethan had learned.

Similarly, and by sheer repetition, the process of *The Query* had evolved from hesitation and uncertainty to a quiet enthusiasm. The technique had become routine: break the ice with light conversation; using the card, share my name and pique their interest with the subject, *The Query* … *a book project*; explain the premise based on another book and its question about hope; leaf through the pages of handwritten notes, pausing to write their name on the next empty page as they watch; probe, listen, and gather the next story. Importantly, to satisfy my own curiosity had it not surfaced, to gently probe the place of faith in the story of their lives.

And listen. With gentleness and respect, listen.

Aside from the tactics unique to *The Query*, early on I had adopted two other practices which perhaps helped to encourage the willingness to share matters closely-held: 1) periodically in the conversation, pausing to restate pieces of their story from my notes, to test whether their intent had been captured correctly, and 2) to refrain from comments about the unfolding story which might be interpreted as judgment. My task was to listen, to gather their reason for hope.

Nine stories have been highlighted in this section entitled **Listening**. During *The Query* most of the stories were of the 'easy listening' nature, like long bike rides on level ground. Not so in the next section, **Engaged**, where at some point the storyteller became the questioner. But that is for the next section.

Back to **Listening**. It is true that every person has a story and that every story is worthy of listening. Yet throughout the months and years of *The Query* project, I became intrigued to engage persons when they might add variety from the demographic mix … e.g., race, age, gender, marital status, vocation, faith experience, etc.

And so, these brief insights on the preceding stories.

Invasive Love. Many would observe that the status of women in American culture has improved markedly over the last half century. And it has. Yet sadly in today's world, women must remain on high alert: aware of surroundings with eyes diverted; cautious to engage in conversation with unknown men in unfamiliar settings. Understandably then, Teresa was slow to engage. She – an attractive young Latina; I – an older, bearded white man, a stranger.

'Ask the question, Larry.' Gently and with respect, engage and guide the conversation to the reason for hope. Set aside the cultural taboos and ask the question. Listen to her story. A second-generation U.S. citizen, poised to enter medical school, in relationship with one of a different race but fearful of broaching that with a father steeped in tradition. Generational roots in the Catholic tradition of the Christian faith, but perhaps not so deeply rooted after all.

Get past the cultural taboos and listen. Just listen.

Two-by-Four. By outward appearance, Stephen was a successful businessman in the twilight of his career. Trim, thinning silver hair fashionably in place, clean shaven and bespectacled, well-tailored blazer and slacks, polished penny loafers. In American culture, one enjoying the privilege of the patriarchal white male.

Probe and listen.

Favorites. A bubbly teenager in the glow of young love, Lacey has yet to learn or apply the cautionary behavior of an older woman when engaging a stranger. Will life's experiences lead her there? Probably. But for purposes of *The Query*, what is hope in the life of a 16-year-old?

Unresolved. Though feeling estranged from the church because of divorce and remarriage, Sharon takes solace from foundational faith practices learned long ago. And in pondering the reason for hope she has perhaps been compelled to reengage with an emotionally distant son.

Principled Living. An immigrant from eastern Europe, a childhood in the grip of communism, an unfolding career with a large Fortune 500 company, and an eagerness to embrace America. Rabur's story contributes a most unique perspective.

Everything Changed. Caring for an aging parent in the grip of dementia can take its toll. Kris' appreciation for husband Todd, and his appreciation for her, make it a little easier to endure the rough stretches of life. It was a joy to witness the quiet comfort they share.

Balance in life is an important precept for Cliff. Very important. Except when it comes to matters spiritual. "I just don't see the need for it" may be an important insight. Will there come a time when Cliff discovers church or faith as a source of balance when things unravel?

Physics & Astrology. It is always a delight to encounter someone like Nate – a person with an infectious enthusiasm. Our time together though brief was memorable, and underscored by his follow up letter. Clearly, the conversation around hope remained with him long afterward. A blessing received, indeed.

Broken Trust is a story which almost wasn't. It proved to be one of the last stories gathered. I was tired after several days away from home and looking forward to a quiet flight and some sleep. *The Query* was not before me. But a big-rig long haul truck driver? Here was a demographic segment un-queried.

Gently, and with respect. It was in answer to the question about the role of faith in his life that the pain and depth of Charlie's story unfolded – a deeply moving story. And in *Broken Trust*, the realization of the indescribable privilege of being alongside another at their most vulnerable. Some call it the 'ministry of presence'. Simply to be alongside, nothing more. The ministry of presence.

The more Charlie shared, the more helpless I felt. No profound words of comfort came to me. Only silence, and listening. Thoughts went through my mind as the pain creased his face in the telling. Do I offer a prayer? What words would provide comfort? Yet it seemed that all I could do was listen. Gently and respectfully, listen. Maybe a ministry of presence was all that was needed. I don't know. I may never know.

His words echoed for days afterward, and still do. The day after the flight, I jotted a note to Charlie expressing encouragement in his journey. I've yet to hear from him. Someday, maybe. But for now, prayer. There is a reason God put *The Query* before me. Maybe for Charlie, it was to be a part of his healing.

Nine stories woven into the vibrant tapestry of American culture. Stories where hope is alive in uniquely different ways. The stories required attentive and careful listening. They didn't require much of me as the listener.

Indeed, long rides are fun when the way is easy.

V. *Engaged*

He learned by watching.

Older boys would fly past astride their bicycles, upright and pumping with their full weight on the pedals to deliver more power. They made it look so easy, climbing those hills. Ethan learned by watching. Soon he gained confidence to stand on the pedals too, shifting from side to side to gain speed more quickly or to climb that hill.

He had long since mastered the basics. "Come on, Grampa," he yelled. "I'll race you to the top," as he sped ahead. I smiled as he pulled away. With practice and learning from others, he had gained confidence ... no longer the novice.

Turns out, it wasn't scary after all.

Engaged are encounters where the storyteller flips roles by posing questions and I, the listener, am unexpectedly nudged to tell my story.

Always 'Always'	149
Critical Analysis	158
Shattered Dream	171
A Common Basis	185
Brokenness	194

Always 'Always'

*"In his mind a man plans his course,
but the Lord directs his steps."*
Proverbs 16:9 (NAB)

When you wait until the last minute, you pay the price on airline travel. This was one of those: inflated ticket price; around-the-country routing for best fares; the dreaded middle seat.

The logic of connecting through Seattle for a Sacramento-to-Tennessee itinerary would befuddle any seasoned traveler. A 2 hour first-leg taking me further from my destination seemed absurd. But when you wait until the last minute …

He was settled into the window seat, intently focused on the tarmac activity. Since the plane was overbooked, the middle seat would be full. No sense watching folks come down the aisle. He would learn of his traveling companion soon enough.

Seemingly aloof to boarding passengers, he proved to be quite engaging once settled. Maybe there was going to be a gem in this Sacramento-Seattle leg after all. We were similar in age and height, but he was more muscular and so had a little more heft to his build. The flight would be cozy.

"My name is Ken," he said as he offered his hand. "What's yours? No sense being strangers if we're gonna be beside each other for a while." His grip was strong, his hand swallowing mine.

And so, out came my card and, "My name is Larry." He studied the card for a moment as I explained it. He was intrigued about the concept of *The Query* and that it was rooted in this book I've been reading, a book of writings from several authors and one of them suggesting the query.

"So, what's the question?"

Because our time together was barely underway, I explained that normally I start by learning about a person's history so that when the question comes I have a better understanding of how life experiences may have shaped the answer. "So, Ken, if you're ok with this, let me learn a little about you first and make a few notes," I suggested, reaching for *The Query* notebook and a pen.

"You want me to tell you all about myself, and then you're gonna ask me a question?" he said. "I want to know the question first." We'd moved from engaging to skeptical.

No problem. Either a story will unfold, or it won't – and if it doesn't, that means a two-hour flight to catch up on some casual reading long postponed.

So, the query: *What is the reason for the hope within you?*

Ken was quiet. He studied me for a bit. "That's the question?" he mused. "I thought this was gonna be something serious. That's the book project?"

"Yeah," I replied. "Well, it's not a book yet. So far it's just a collection of stories people have shared, all captured in this little notebook. And I must say, each person's story is moving. Some are long; some are short. But they are all pretty moving." I was slowly flipping through the pages of handwritten notes; Ken was watching with interest.

"So you ask the question, and I answer it. Is that it?"

"Yep. I ask the question, and you answer it. But what usually happens is your answer will lead to conversation. And through that I get a sense of how your answer has been shaped by your life. But you won't have to share anything you don't want to. I'm just collecting stories. That's it."

He studied me again. "What's your game? What's in this for you?"

I chuckled. "There ain't anything in this for me. When we're done and if you're interested, I'll share how this all began. The only thing in it for me is to listen to stories – powerful stories."

He hesitated. Then, "Ok … you ask the question. I answer, and then you ask some more questions? And I can stop answering questions anytime I want to?"

"That's right – those are the rules. You're in control."

For the first time, Ken had brought me face-to-face with the flip side of Peter's caution when answering the question: ... *and do so with gentleness and respect.* The experience with Ken was making it very clear that doing so with 'gentleness and respect' is as important in *posing* the question as it is in answering it.

The preliminary jousting was over. "Ok," Ken agreed. "Go ahead, ask the question. And I'll stop when I want to."

"Here's what the guy wrote in this book," I continued. *"Always be prepared to give the answer to the question, when somebody asks you, of the reason for the hope within you ... and do so with gentleness and respect.* So, that's the question. *What is the reason for the hope that is within you?"*

Ken's demeanor changed from tussling to thoughtful.

"There is no reason. It just is. I'm not sure it is as much hope, as confidence. If something isn't ok today, I'll make it ok tomorrow. I am constantly finding ways to improve. That's my natural curiosity. Always finding ways to get things done. Refusing to let things get in the way.

"There is no 'can't'. There is always 'always'. There is always a way. You've just got to find it."

Once they began, the words came quickly. There is a sense of confidence about Ken, a sense of 'get it done'. My kind of guy. A man's man.

Ken was born in the wine country, joining three older sisters. At age 5, his family moved from their valley farm to a home in Oak Park, a tiny suburb on the south edge of Sacramento city. For years, Oak Park had the reputation as one of the tougher neighborhoods in Sacramento.

"I had a lot of conflict in those early years, mostly because I was a farm boy moving to town. When I was 11, my folks sent me to live with an older sister in the Northwest for about a year. While I was with her, they moved out of Oak Park to Carmichael. When I came back home, I came home to Carmichael.

"In the 1960's, Carmichael was a middle and upper-middle class suburb east of Sacramento. It's still one of the nicer communities. Life was uneventful.

"College wasn't for me, so at 19 I joined the Army. It was either enlist or be drafted. I figured if I enlisted, maybe I'd be able to have a better chance at learning a trade."

And a trade he learned during an 18-month tour in Vietnam. Ken became a communications specialist as a Tactical Microwave Systems Repairman setting up microwave towers on hilltops.

He was eager to get back and turn his trade into a career. But returning Vietnam veterans didn't always have an easy go. He approached the electrical union to sign on as an apprentice electrician.

"They told me I'd never be an electrician in that town because I didn't have the right 'connections' with the union. I guess I had to be invited by someone already in the union, but I didn't know anybody."

Disillusioned, he roamed the country for a year.

"When I got back, there was a strike going on in a nearby manufacturing plant. I needed a job. So, I crossed the picket line as a scab to get started so I could be an electrician apprentice."

Eventually he found an electrician job with a contractor; they were wiring grocery stores. "The foremen were alcoholics. It was tough. But I stuck with it, and when they all got fired I joined the union and became the job foreman at 23. I haven't been out of work since, almost forty years later."

As the years went by, Ken constantly worked to improve himself, constantly studying. "The union asked me to put together a course to teach how to run conduits. I became a superintendent for a prison job and then a project manager for 13 years, all as a union member. I was proud of that, because usually you must leave the union to be a project manager.

"Eventually I got on a large power plant job as the superintendent. I enjoy large projects, bringing them in on-time and under budget."

The conversation turned from career to family.

He married at age 30. "That lasted about nine years, and I have a daughter from that. Then in a relationship for 5 years, raising someone else's teenagers. Not fun!"

After a bout of singleness and coming up empty, he tried Match.com and met Ginny. "We've been married 6 years, and I've never been so happy. Gin has three children and a stepchild. They're good kids, and we're very close," he smiled.

The conversation paused while note-taking caught up. There were already several pages.

I studied what had been written so far, and then braced to continue. This part of *The Query* is always a little dicey because it is difficult to predict how one will react. Given the way our conversation began, I was a little apprehensive.

Ken was studying me as I studied the notes.

"You know, Ken, I'd like to revisit what you shared earlier, sort of your life philosophy. Here's what I've heard you say, or at least it's what I've written down:

If something isn't ok today, I'll make it ok tomorrow ... always finding ways to get things done...refusing to let things get in the way ... there is no 'can't'. There is always 'always'. There is always a way. You've just got to find it.

"Did I get that right?"

"Yeah," he said, with a twinkle in his eye. "That's pretty much how I look at things."

"Well, I'm wondering. Who were some of the people who shaped that view of life for you? Who were the significant influencers?"

He turned to the window, thinking – and then, "My 'life philosophy', as you call it, was mostly shaped by those who tried to stop me, people who told me I couldn't do something. If somebody said 'no', I was determined to do it. I was an Eagle Scout, and that was good for me. I was always a stubborn kid who did things my way."

His dad grew up in the South and was an electrician. He went on to college, became an industrial engineer, and eventually ran a civilian department at an Air Force base in California. Both parents died some time ago.

We were quiet for a while. "So when you're not doing your job, what do you like to do?"

He was passionate about off-roading for a long time, but as the years have passed he finds he enjoys their home in the Northwest where he built a 40'x60' shop. He likes to tinker with woodworking tools that belonged to his dad, and some automotive tools for his four-wheel drive, and a trove of electrical tools. He and Ginny have a motor home; they enjoy traveling.

"But when I'm in the middle of a project, it takes all my time. I enjoy problem solving. Right now, I'm working on a huge silicon manufacturing plant that makes beads for use in photovoltaic cells. There's a gas manufacturing plant alongside and we're just finishing up the job. I've been there 18 months as the job superintendent overseeing 470 electricians."

Now, the riskiest part of *The Query*: the introduction of 'faith' as a topic for the conversation if it hasn't come up. With Ken, it hadn't.

I shared that the book I'd referenced at the outset was the Bible, and that the author was Peter, one of Jesus' twelve disciples.

Not surprisingly, Ken reacted. "Oh, so you're a religious guy! I should have known."

Gently and with respect. I've learned that with Ken.

"What does that mean, a 'religious' guy?" I asked. "I don't know that I'm 'religious', but, yes, my faith is an important part of my life."

Ken's response was quick, almost abrupt, and fast-paced. "I don't believe in organized religion." He stopped and watched as I wrote. I wanted to be sure I captured his words as he said them. He seemed surprised.

Then he continued. "I do believe there is something out there that is bigger than me, and that there is probably an afterlife. But organized religion fills you with bullshit and tries to get money out of you."

I was writing, word for word. He was watching, word for word. Surprised and satisfied at his words on paper, he turned reflective. "I do have a faith inside me, I guess. But I don't know that the faith inside me is a primary driver. In fact, I don't think it is. It's just in the background.

"I have made it my business to get better and better in the electrical business. That is what drives me."

I asked whether church was a part of his life, and learned that his folks were devout Mormons, up to their deaths. "They tried to get me into it, but I got my first job when I was 14 and stopped going to church. After a while, they gave up and quit arguing with me about it. My younger sister is a 'born again', and my older sister married a Mormon."

The flight was ending, and so the conversation. I asked Ken if he would be willing to share his contact information should I want to get in touch with him as the book unfolded.

"Sure," he replied. "But if you send me any church crap, I'm gonna throw it out!" We both laughed.

As we shook hands at parting, his closing words were a compliment of sorts. He looked me in the eye and said, "I enjoyed the conversation. It was good to talk about things we don't normally talk about."

Indeed.

A story shared ... a blessing received.

Insights: *Always 'Always'*

The encounter with Ken was challenging and fun. And as it turned out, enriching. But enriching in a way the story doesn't reflect. To explain, this excerpt from near the end of his story:

> I shared that the book I'd referenced at the outset was the Bible, and that the author was Peter, one of Jesus' twelve disciples.
>
> Not surprisingly, Ken reacted. "Oh, so you're a religious guy! I should have known."
>
> Gently and with respect. I've learned that with Ken. "What does that mean, a 'religious' guy?" I asked.
>
> "I don't know that I'm 'religious', but, yes, my faith is an important part of my life."

The Christian faith has been central to shaping my view of life. For as long as I can remember, church as the place where believers gather and encourage each other has been matter of fact. In darkest times, the community of believers has sustained me. Not every believer. Sometimes, hardly any. But almost always, it has been a Christ-follower who has walked alongside. Cried with me. Encouraged me.

Because faith and church as community have been central to that, it is easy for me to engage in conversations about God, or Jesus, or the power of the Spirit in settings where others share similar views. But beyond those walls, with persons who don't know me in those settings? There lies my great discomfort! Is it my Midwest piety?

No. It is fear. Fear that someone will take me to task on this 'God mystery'. That in embracing the 'God mystery', I may be belittled. And if there were ever someone who would do it, it would be Ken – a cynic if ever there was one. Indeed, with his reaction and his earlier bluster, belittlement could easily have been next: "Oh, so you're a religious guy! I should have known."

Perhaps many of *The Query* stories had affected me. I don't know. But at that moment with Ken, there was neither hesitation nor fear. Instead, spoken as a quiet but firm certainty: "… but, yes, my faith is an important part of my life." No fancy theology, no cerebral 'wow'. Just a simple, public declaration of truth. My faith, this Christ-following faith, *is* an important part of my life.

And here's the miracle: Ken did *not* belittle me. Oh yes, he belittled church and organized religion. But he didn't belittle *me*. It seems I had experienced what bicyclist Ethan had already learned: Turns out, it wasn't scary after all.

A couple years later, as the encounter with Ken came off the notebook pages and became *Always 'Always'*, I couldn't help but again recall Jesus' encouragement to the Twelve as he sent them out:

> …*do not worry about what to say or how to say it. At that time, you will be given what to say, for it will not be you speaking, but the Spirit of your Father speaking through you.* (Matthew 10:19b-20)

The words spoken to Ken were not inspiring. But they were inspired for that moment. Of that I am certain.

One last tidbit about Ken. When his story joined the others as the first draft of *The Query*, I called the phone number he had given me to ask whether his physical address was still correct. As with others, I wanted to test whether the recreated story was reasonably true to the conversation. After introducing myself and reminding him of the airline encounter, he chuckled. He was surprised to hear from me, saying that he had figured the whole experience had been some kind of scam. We both laughed. "Sure," he said. "Send it to me. And if I feel like it, I'll send it back." Not surprising, given his threat to throw out any church crap!

Months went by, and then the return envelope with *The Query* draft inside. At the bottom of my explanatory cover letter was his one-word handwritten scrawl: "Thanks."

Through the encounter with Ken, I have been enriched.

Critical Analysis

"Flesh into bread, blood into wine
Not this time"
from *Battles Waste*, a poem of war

The conversation began casually.

We had both settled into the start of a long flight, this nonstop from Sacramento to Washington DC/Dulles, each intent on what was before us. With an empty seat between, the rare extra room was an uncommon treat. It promised to be one of those leisurely flights with plenty of time to catch up on some long postponed reading.

He was friendly, though somewhat clipped in his presence. He seemed purposeful, matter of fact. Late forties, perhaps; trim and well groomed. His casual dress belied a professional bearing.

He was immersed in the reading material before him. Pushed to the side of his tray table with the spine facing me, a paperback book caught my eye: *The Penguin Book of First World War Poetry* (edited by Jon Silkim, 2nd edition). I was intrigued by the title. His attention was elsewhere.

"Would you mind if I look at that book?" I leaned over and asked. "It is an interesting title. Is it poetry from World War I?"

His face lit up. "Sure," he smiled, and handed it to me. I glanced at the contents, noticing it was a collection of short poems by many different authors, each name followed by a parenthetical.

"Are these numbers in the parentheses their lifetimes?" If so, many of the endings would clearly have been during the war. Endings of 1915, 1916, 1917.

"Yes," he replied. "It's a collection of poems from soldiers during that war. Quite a few were written on the front lines. Many were killed in action. They were all British soldiers." He pointed to several poems which he found moving, and I turned to them. He was correct, they were very moving – so much so, that I decided to buy a copy another day.

He began to tell the stories of several the authors. Clearly, he had a deep grasp of things military. Noting his short-cropped hair and athletic build, I asked, "Are you in the military?"

"Yes sir, 25 years. I'm due to retire next year, and then on to private life."

What then?

"Not sure. I'm beginning to think about that, but I have plenty of time."

His story began to unfold. He hopes to retire as a lieutenant colonel before turning 50. His career has spanned the globe, with two tours in Iraq, and tours in Afghanistan, Bosnia, Haiti, Central America, and Mexico. His specialty? "I'm a career officer ... the Army has been my life."

"Ah, I see. So, there are probably some things you've experienced that you can't talk about."

"Oh yeah, there are some things I can't tell you," his eyes twinkled. "But there's a lot that was just the same for everybody."

He was returning from a visit to his small home town in California. After high school, he earned a BA in international studies from a nearby university. That was followed by advanced studies at the Marian Institute. An older brother owns a small business; a younger brother is a forensic investigator.

While attending college and early in his Army career, he met and later married Elizabeth, "and we've been blessed with four sons and two daughters." The kids range from 15 (twin daughters, adopted at 18 months) to 23 years of age.

"My dad was a federal agent who grew up in the Midwest, and Mom was from southern California." Elizabeth grew up in southern California, too, with two younger brothers.

"Well," I chuckled, "I can see why Elizabeth wanted to adopt some girls. The poor gal had been surrounded by guys!" He nodded and laughed.

With all those tours of duty, he had spent a lot of time away from family. "Your wife must be a very strong and resourceful person. How has that worked out?"

"Yes, I've been very fortunate. Elizabeth is a very supportive wife, a good mother, and a great homemaker. Usually when I was away, she would go back close to her home and get support from her family. They are very close-knit." He's now stationed in Texas, where they're together and where he expects to finish out his career.

"So, how did you and the family endure the time apart?"

He turned thoughtful for a moment. Then, "You don't 'endure'. At least, I don't think you endure it. You just deal with it."

He asked what I did for a living. I related the early years in the corporate world and the last twenty or so in executive search, and offered to be available to him as he nears retirement – perhaps in some way being helpful if private industry beckons. We exchanged names and shook hands as he slipped my business card into his pocket.

"Frank, if you don't mind, I'd like to explain a project I'm working on, leading to a book." I reached into the backpack and pulled out *The Query* notebook, showing him the pages of notes chronicling the stories of people over the last couple years. After explaining the premise, I continued, "Would you mind if I made some notes, and then asked a few questions?"

"I don't mind," he smiled. "But I don't have much of a story to tell. You're not going to find anything of interest in my life."

"Well, we'll see. So far, I've been amazed at everybody's story. They've all been quite interesting. I just regret I waited so long in life to start this. It is fascinating!"

Yes, he confirmed, the life of the military meant a lot of moving around, living all over. And time apart.

"Where would the kids call 'home'?"

"Oh, they would probably say that California is their home. That's where they feel the most settled. That was always the 'place to come home to' while I was stationed overseas. That strong family support network has been a real blessing."

"With so much time apart," I probed, "how did you and Elizabeth stay, you know, 'connected'?"

"When I was in Desert Storm, the first Iraq war, it was tough. Letters and the occasional phone call. At the AT&T phone tent, to wait your turn for a ten-minute call often meant two hours of standing in line. But that ten minutes was everything. By the time my second tour in Iraq came around, e-mail was common so it was much easier to feel connected. And in Afghanistan … well, Skype made it even easier."

We talked of current events, like the complete draw-down of troops underway in Iraq and his thoughts, at least as far as he felt comfortable sharing. He became critical of the politics of the situation, concerned that decisions around Iraq and Afghanistan were being driven by the political climate in the U.S. and not by the situations in either country. He seemed dismayed that the effect of 'all eyes on the 2012 election' seemed to be dictating policy, rather than policy being dictated by reality.

Do you believe others in the military share those views or concerns?

"Oh, yes, but no one will speak openly of it beyond the military circle. But let's be clear. No one questions the hierarchy and the place of the Commander in Chief. We all respect that and we implement policy as directed. But there is a deep fear that things will unravel quickly in Iraq, and then what? Folks at home wouldn't stand for a recommitment of ground troops there. And so, we walk away. We're worried for the folks we're leaving behind, for those deep friendships with Iraqis who put their lives on the line to help the coalition forces on the ground. Those folks now fear for their lives, with good cause. They are at huge risk and probably many of them will just disappear, never to be heard from again.

"And so, for what? There is a sadness that we've sacrificed so much there. For what? How do you have the conversation with the families of soldiers who didn't come back?"

What about Afghanistan?

"Not much different. The decision to draw down is political, with an eye to the election."

There seemed a thread of skepticism in his persona, almost quiet resignation. A long career ending with what to show? A sense of sadness, it seemed.

It didn't seem fruitful to go any further with that. There was little Frank or I could do about the macro-decisions of government. There was nothing to resolve between us. I was just listening.

"In any event, thank you for your service. Thanks very much." He shook my hand in appreciation.

We returned to the query ... *the reason for the hope within*. Earlier I had shared that at some point during the flight, this would be the question I would pose.

"I've been struggling with your question for a while and not just now because you've asked it, though I've not heard it put quite that way before. When you're at the end of a job, a 25-year career, you wonder. But tomorrow will always be better than yesterday. It always has been. My kids are already better than I am.

"My hope has to be centered around my kids. The only hope I really have is that I've done well for them." He turned quiet, reflective.

How, or where, have you experienced hope during your career?

"Oh, I've had some interesting times, for sure.

"In October 1989 I was with a tank battalion in Germany. Czech refugees were streaming into Germany. We were waiting for the Russians to come across the Rhine. So, we grabbed some cases of Budweiser, a bunch of hamburgers and some ice cream, and had a party for the Czech refugees. I'll never forget one of them. Over and over, he sang *The Killer*, by Jerry Lee Lewis – over and over. How in the world, behind the Iron Curtain, had he learned a song from Jerry Lee Lewis? It struck me, the ways people find hope.

"In Port-au-Prince (Haiti), we were on our way to a communication tower at the top of a mountain. A little old man walked in front of the Humvee and as we slowly crawled past him, he tapped on my window. I told the driver to stop. We got out. He looked in my eyes with tears in his, and cried, 'Thank God for President Clinton. He gave us liberty.'

"A lady in Bosnia, in 1994, also praised President Clinton 'for bringing safety and security into our lives.'

"In Afghanistan, my thoughts go to Billy. Billy is about eighteen, a Shi'ite. We worked side-by-side every day for 6 months. He was my interpreter. All he wanted was to go to the U.S. so he could study law and come back home to rebuild his country. And he has. I understand he's in Arizona in his third year of studies. I.C.E. has helped him. Billy has hope.

"In Iraq, I worked closely with an Iraqi major who wanted to visit the U.S. Now, because we're walking away, he knows he'll never get here. He has lost hope."

His stories wove from one to the other at a rapid clip. I asked Frank to stop for a bit, to rest my hand. We sat for a while in silence. I was reflecting on his story, unable to imagine his life experiences. Here, on an airplane high above the Midwest, listening to his story. To his 'uninteresting' story!

Then, we started again.

"I'm curious, Frank. You've had life experiences that are quite different from most people you encounter now, and especially as you leave military life. To what extent has 'faith' shaped your outlook? How has 'faith' been a part of hope for you?"

He sat quietly for a few moments, staring into the seatback in front of him. Then quietly, "Faith is another one of those places where hope is lost to some degree, because when I banked over twenty years in the Catholic church, then the scandal in the church in the '90s ...", his voice trailed off. He looked at me. "Well, there went my hope from the church. Faith isn't a place for hope."

I wanted to be sure I understood. "Was there something that happened at your church? I want to make sure I understand what you mean."

"No," he replied. "Just all that stuff with abuse of boys by the priests, everywhere. For months at a time as more stories unfolded, the church was silent. No acknowledgement that the church, the priests, were wrong. It was wrong. Everything about it was wrong, and the church was silent. The church would probably be silent today if the stories hadn't become public. It was wrong – and when the church fails you … ", his voice trailed off again. Then, "It failed me. And then, shaped by later years from 2001 on, for months at a time there was no acknowledgement that the church was wrong."

I let his words sit in silence, pondering his sharing and my sense of him.

"It seems that you carry a healthy amount of skepticism in your outlook on things," I observed. "You're skeptical of the course of the military, of the influence of politics on matters military. You sound skeptical of the church. Does that skepticism show itself in other ways?"

Frank sat in thought for a bit. Then, "No, I don't think I'm a skeptic. Maybe 'critical analysis' more so than skepticism. I've been trained, or at least I've learned, that you must be critical in your analysis in the business I'm in. So perhaps it has made me more critical of things. Maybe I see with a different eye than most."

"I wonder, Frank, about this faith thing," I offered, gingerly. "I wonder if your 'critical analysis' works when it comes to your experience with 'church'. Where are you today, with 'church'? Are you involved in 'church'? Or is your family?"

"No. I haven't been back to church since. It's not for me."

What about Elizabeth? Where is she in all of it?

He thought for a moment. "I guess you could say she's on 'pause'. She hasn't been very active, and I don't know how much of that is because of me or whether that is how she feels. Maybe she'll re-engage. Our boys have found a place, a nondenominational Christian church which has been good for them. But I don't know whether I'll ever make it back."

There was silence while note-taking caught up.

"Well," I continued, "I'm wondering about something. Maybe you can help me. It seems to me that in this faith thing, this Christian faith, that a 'critical assessment' could lead you to separate the faith into two parts. Maybe there are others, but it seems to me, two parts. One part would be what we could call the 'institutional church' – and by that, I mean that part of the faith that is of human construct. And then there's the other part, the Jesus part. The belief in this 'Jesus as God among us' part. You know, Emmanuel, 'God with us' (it was that time of year when the Christmas season was approaching).

"It seems to me that if we can separate the faith into these two pieces, maybe it's easier to understand our frustration with the faith. Maybe it's our frustration with the 'human piece' of it and not the 'Jesus piece'. We are, after all, flawed. So, it shouldn't be any surprise that those human flaws find a home in the church, too.

"And so, I'm wondering whether your 'critical assessment' is focused on the shortcomings of the human piece. At your core, at your center, what about the deeper aspect of the faith? What about the 'Jesus piece'? As a Christian, as a follower of Jesus, where is that piece of the faith?"

Frank was quiet. Thoughtful.

"You're right," he reflected. "I'd not thought of the two aspects of faith that way. I guess I'd always thought of 'church' and 'faith' as one. But now that you put it that way, yes, it's true that my disappointment is with the 'church' piece. Not Jesus. I think that part of faith for me hasn't changed."

"You know," I observed, "It seems to me that the Catholic tradition places a high emphasis on both the 'institution' of the church – its tradition, and the magisterium (the priesthood and the Vatican) – as well as the Bible as the Word of God. Yes, the scandals in the church have been awful. They've been awful not just for the Catholic church, but for all expressions of Christian tradition. All churches have suffered, whether from skepticism or cynicism, and that is understandable. Yet somehow I wonder if we can walk away from the 'Jesus' piece, the God piece.

"So the question is, how do we see past the human failings and continue to grow deeper in our understanding of God? How do we keep God at our center when the church seems to be the last place to look for God?"

Slowly, with sincerity, Frank replied. "I hadn't thought of it that way. It's something to think about."

"I've become convinced," I continued, "as my own church expression has struggled with disagreement or interpretation of God's word – with divisions over whose interpretations are right or wrong – I'm convinced that it's all the work of the evil one. The devil, Satan, knows just how to wedge his way into the pieces of our human disagreement or our human behavior to cause us to walk away from the church. And in doing that, to walk away from the faith … well, then the devil wins.

"And that is sad. The world needs people who believe in God and who live out that faith. It's where hope comes in. And that takes us full circle, back to the query: *what is the reason for the hope that is within you?* And I've got to believe that, somewhere, there's this Jesus piece of faith that is still at your center, too."

Frank turned quiet. He was thoughtful for a long while.

The pilot announced the approach to Dulles. Tray tables up, seat backs to upright positions, books and notebooks stowed.

As Frank stood to claim his overhead gear, he handed me his card. "Could we stay in touch? I'd like to."

What will become of this conversation, I wondered while meandering through Dulles to baggage claim? I don't know. I don't know.

But I do know this. This project, this Query thing, has opened doors to genuine and deep conversations around faith in ways I could never have imagined. I don't know why. All I know is, it has. And I am being blessed.

All because of a Bible verse which caused such consternation.

Frank and I did e-connect over the next few months as he sought advice on the transition into civilian employment. Some time passed. And then, almost a year to the day after that long flight, an e-mail arrived:

To: Larry
From: Frank COL USARMY (US)
Subject: ⏎Re: 'Hi' back atchya ...
Date Sent: Tue 11/27/2012 6:06:43 PM

> Larry,
>
> I reenlisted for another year. Crazy I know. But soon. Gives me a chance to work on my war poetry- here is one for your book
>
> <u>Battles Waste</u>
>
> Pull him down the Sergeant said
> And we scampered to the wire
> The body still moist and tie-dyed crimson
> Flesh into bread, blood into wine
> Not this time
> only medical waste splashed about
> the stretcher bearers face
>
> I love Tennessee- spent a few years there at Fort Campbell. Great state.
>
> Frank

A story shared ... a blessing received.

Insights: *Critical Analysis*

Each encounter in *The Query* has been memorable in its own way. Reflecting on the experience with Frank, two preeminent themes in military tradition come to mind: honor and respect. Every aspect of Frank's bearing conveyed honor. Every word and facial expression conveyed respect.

Military tradition holds that uniform and rank receive respect, whether merited by the person within. After his lengthy and honorable service, Frank brings that tradition of respect to the world. Extending respect to the other has become a part of his nature. Our dialogue was respectful. Perhaps it was this mutual respect which opened the door to his thoughts as the conversation turned to faith.

By the time of *Critical Analysis*, the process of *The Query* had been underway for several years. The pattern and technique had become second nature. The feeling of uncertainty in exploring faith as a dimension in one's living was long gone. Instead, exploring faith had become a natural part of the process and an essential piece in the understanding of the other. With Frank, it was beautiful in its unfolding. The query of faith prompted his characterization of 'critical analysis' as central to his outlook. Not skepticism nor cynicism, but critical analysis. What a marvelous door opener to the follow-on question, i.e., the application of his training (critical analysis) to his struggle with the church.

Readers of the first draft of *Critical Analysis* have asked what prompted me to disaggregate faith into the two parts, i.e., the church part as distinct from the Jesus part. Beyond being an inspiration in the moment, it is unexplainable. In hindsight, it is not surprising. Those inspirations have been a thread all along.

Living brings conflict and tension. Therapists hold that dealing effectively with them includes developing the ability to step back and identify their source. The most difficult tensions in my life have arisen when a shift in closely-held values occur. When the shift in values occurs in minuscule increments, it may take some time for tension to build to the point of commanding attention. When a shift is rapid, the tension can explode without warning. We all can point to such situations. They arise in the home, in the family, in the world of work or school – often among those we hold dear. And yes, even in the church, within the community of faith.

Frank's lament is understandable. In Christian tradition when one is set apart through vows of ordination, he (or she, in some traditions) receives a sacred if unspoken trust by the community. Egregious conduct undermines or fractures that trust. Persons, whether victim or witness, are hurt. Depending on how it is addressed, broken trust can permeate the community. At times the hurt may extend beyond the immediate community into the larger society.

The flurry of media reports of priests engaged in aberrant behavior unsettled Frank. The stonewalling by the institutional hierarchy to the breadth and depth of the problem betrayed his trust in the church. And so, he had moved on, and away, from 'church'.

Our encounter came during the season of Advent. In churches of liturgical tradition, Advent begins around December 1 and ends with Christmas. It is a season of spiritual reflection and preparation when believers recall the significance of the birth of the Christ child – of Emmanuel, 'God with us'. For me, the several weeks of Advent are usually a time for more intentional reflection on God in the world, on God in my life. So perhaps the turn in the conversation with Frank was an inevitable confluence of any number of things. But assuredly, 'God with us' in the person of Jesus is central to my walk in the Christian faith and is heightened as Christmas nears.

Frank's lament was, however, more than deep sorrow. It had become revulsion of the church, and repulsion from it. And I get it. I confess to harboring moments of revulsion and deep disgust with the church when actions seem to seek solely to preserve the institution, the status quo. Worse, there have been times when I have been a part of the crowd, clamoring for that status quo. And there have been times when I have been tempted to walk away, never to return.

But it is, for me, the Jesus piece – the 'God with us' piece – which then discomforts me and keeps me centered. It is through Jesus' own disgust with the institutional church of his day that the 'God mystery', the Jesus piece, encourages me. Often it comes much later in times of quiet, usually with open journal before me and pen in hand. In moving past those times of lament and disgust, the words of Paul to the early church are always a helpful reminder: *"encourage one another, and build each other up."* (1 Thessalonians 5:11)

Suggesting that Frank apply 'critical analysis' to help him reconnect with the Jesus piece at his core was my way of encouraging him. The sacramental phrase within his subsequent poem, *Battles Waste*, makes me believe that he has.

Thanks be to God.

Shattered Dream

"Why do you see the speck in your neighbor's eye, but do not notice the log in your own eye? Or how can you say to your neighbor, 'Let me take the speck out of your eye,' while the log is in your own eye? You hypocrite, first take the log out of your own eye, and then you will see clearly to take the speck out of your neighbor's eye."
Matthew 7:3-5 (NRSV)

"I'm on my way to a weeklong training session in Chicago," she smiled, "so I guess it's visiting."

'Are you going home or going visiting?' is my common icebreaker with seatmates on a long flight. We had just departed Sacramento; my connecting flight was through O'Hare airport.

She was petite with long dark hair flattering her dark eyes, dressed comfortably for air travel in stylish jeans, casual top and light jacket. Her welcoming smile suggested that an engaging conversation might be in the offing. As the plane gained altitude, I settled into the *Sacramento Bee* to catch up on news of the hometown from which I had moved a few months before. This had been my first return visit. The 10 days had flown by, reconnecting with friendships spanning 24 years. Yet, I was looking forward to getting back to my new home in east Tennessee and the needed rest.

Articles of metro news prompted light-hearted chatter. The drama and plight of the re-nested NBA Kings; seemingly endless budget woes of the state government and related political tussling; the foothill fires in the neighboring Sierras which had covered the city and valley with a yellow haze.

Gradually, a personal story began to unfold.

She is 47, and has been with the same high-profile financial services firm for 20 of those years. Work is meaningful, with a quiet pride of company and role. Her husband of 22 years owns a distributorship; they met at Long Beach State where both earned degrees in accounting.

"Both my parents were born in Nogales on the Arizona-Mexico border," she reflected, "and their families moved to Los Angeles when they were kids. They met in L.A., got married and a family came along. I was born in

L.A, and I was the baby. When I was 9, my folks divorced. I have three older sisters and an older brother, from two different moms.

"When I was 11, Mom married again. Eight years later, they divorced. Two years after that, Mom married for the third time, to Sergio. She and Sergio were married for 12 years when Mom died of cancer. She was 56.

"And my dad died from cancer, too, when he was 77."

It had been 4 years since the start of *The Query*, since that moment on the Alaskan tarmac when the extreme discomfort compelled me with *I want you to <u>ask</u> the question … quit worrying about how you're going to answer it. I want you to <u>ask</u> it*. Something about this unfolding story prompted me to wonder about her reason for hope. So once again, out came the notebook, the card, the premise, and the request to listen to her story.

She studied the card, then accepted my outstretched hand. "Hi, Larry," she smiled. "I'm Ellen. It's a pleasure to meet you!" We chuckled, almost as though at this point introductions weren't necessary. "So, what kind of answer are you looking for?" she asked with eyebrow raised.

"Well, let me jot down a few things about your story, and then we'll get to that." She watched patiently, answering questions to fill in the blanks of her story from what had been recalled so far.

"So your mom died from cancer. That had to be tough. How did Sergio and the family deal with that?"

Ellen turned somber. "After Mom died, it came out that Sergio had been sexually molesting my niece, Kathryn, for 5 years. Kathryn was 5 years old when it began; she was molested up to age 10." She paused. "Sergio was arrested, convicted, and jailed. After his ten-year prison term, he was deported back to Mexico." Another pause, and then a smile. "Kathryn is 25 now, soon to be married, and we're planning a bridal shower when I get back. We're so excited!" she beamed.

The conversation turned to her and husband, Steve. "We dated for 4 years in college. Steve was 19 when we met, and I was a junior in college. We waited to get married until he finished college. That was his idea, not mine," she laughed. They moved north and a couple years later, she started work while Steve cut his business teeth.

It wasn't long and she became pregnant. "Today, Sean is 19 and in college in Oregon," she said, the pride apparent. "He wants to be a counselor for middle-school kids."

Six years later, Faith was born. "Faith is 13, loves soccer, is very determined, and very stubborn. There seems to be constant tension between her and me," she sighed. "It's frustrating. I just don't get it. Sean was such an easy kid, no problems. But Faith? Oh, boy! Thank heavens Steve is even-keeled. He calms us down when the shouting starts. I don't know what I'd do without him!" she smiled, as the beam returned.

She sat quietly and watched as the pen scratched across the pages. Then she chuckled. "I guess I don't have to worry about anybody reading your notes, do I?" We laughed, and the pen rested for a bit.

After a few minutes, I continued. "Ellen, tell me about faith. Has that been a part of your life?"

"I was raised Roman Catholic," she replied, "and went to Mass every weekend. That came from Mom. Mom used to tell the story that when she was young, she wanted to get an education so she joined a nunnery. She was a nun for 2 years, and then was asked to rethink her vows. So, she left the nunnery and went into law enforcement. And even though she was twice divorced and the church seemed to turn its back on her, she never left the church. Her faith was important to her, and she was serious about her kids being raised in the church."

By the time college came along, Ellen had gradually fallen away from weekly Mass, instead going to church only on special days like Easter and Christmas. "When Steve and I met, it wasn't a big issue for me. Steve was raised Lutheran, and after we got married we went to church a few times but it didn't become an important part of our lives."

She sat silently for a few moments, and then asked about my faith experience. I shared of also being raised Lutheran, of marriage in the Catholic church but continuing in the Lutheran tradition, of being blessed with three children, in later years the painful journey of divorce – and all the while, a deepening faith.

She sat quietly. It seemed time for the query. But before I could proceed, she began softly, though hesitant.

"A couple months ago, our life took a turn that caught us by surprise. And I'm really struggling with it." She stopped. It was one of those moments when a phrase has been spoken but uncertainty follows – uncertainty whether to continue, or whether to try to retract what has just been said. I sat attentive, silent.

She took a breath and then continued slowly. "A couple months ago, Sean called from college. He and his girlfriend, Laura, needed to come and talk with me about something, so they were on their way home. He didn't want to talk about it on the phone. They wanted to talk with me first, and then together with me to approach Steve for the same conversation. Sean said they'd be arriving in a couple hours.

"I was grateful for the couple hours to prepare and be ready to be the understanding mom and future mother-in-law. So, I was prepared for the 'Mom, we're going to have a baby and get married' news. And I was ok with that. After all, those things are not all that uncommon.

"So the three of us sat down. Even though Sean wasn't smiling and Laura wasn't either, I wasn't ready for what came next.

"No, Laura wasn't pregnant. No, there wasn't going to be a wedding. Instead, they had come to tell me that Sean is gay. Laura started crying. Sean sat and watched me – and I was stunned! I didn't know what to say. I didn't know how to react. I just sat there, stunned.

"Sean continued, 'Mom, I love Laura. And I have a choice: I can choose how to live. But I don't have a choice in being gay. I can choose to get married to Laura and live a 'normal' life, or I can choose to live as a gay man.'"

Ellen shared more about Sean. "He is such a gifted young man, a very talented musician. And he wants the deep emotional attachment he has with

Laura. But he says he has no desire for physical sex and doesn't care if he ever has.

"Laura loves Sean so. But she is struggling because she knows that a relationship in marriage would never be 'whole'. And now she doesn't know whether she will feel 'full' in a relationship knowing that for Sean the sex thing isn't important."

She paused to gather her thoughts.

"Sean shared that the defining moment for him was when he had just gotten to college and he was at a party. There was a girl. They were going to have sex and she asked if he had a condom. He lied and said he didn't, to avoid the sex. And it was then that he realized that the physical attraction was not for her or for any girl.

"Laura said that when he told her, at first she was relieved because she had thought that maybe there was something wrong with her because he wasn't responding to her advances."

It turns out that her husband, Steve, is taking all this far better than Ellen. "He says, 'Would you want Sean to marry, have a family, but never be happy because he couldn't be wholly who he is?'

"And I know he's right. But I know that I'm grieving, and it's very selfish. This is not what I had wanted for my son. I may never have a wonderful daughter-in-law. I may never have a grandchild through him. It has shattered my dream of his future, and of my future."

I had been focused on Ellen and her pain, and had forgotten about notes. Quietly, I picked up the pen and started writing. She sat silently, deep in thought. The notes finished, I put the pen down and sat silently, too.

She turned to me, smiled, and said, "I'll bet that's a new story, huh?" I chuckled softly and noted what a blessing *The Query* experience has been each time a story is shared.

"Has anybody ever said 'no'?" she asked.

"No, not a single person," I replied. "That has been one of the most surprising pieces of this experience. And as their stories unfold, I'm always amazed at the depth of the life experiences they share."

Now, it was time for the query.

"So, Ellen, let's go back to where we began. *What is the reason for the hope within you?*"

"I've been thinking about that," she said. "It's my children. My hope is that they will always be happy, and live their lives the way they want to. Not for anyone else, and especially, not for me. My son was so worried about disappointing me, but he didn't. It was probably the opposite!"

I shared that the book of writings from which the query comes is the Bible, from the first letter attributed to Peter. The conversation returned, then, to faith.

"You know," she said, "Sean asked me a question a couple weeks ago and I couldn't answer it. I felt so helpless. He asked, 'If God created each of us individually, and has a plan and a path for each of us, why did He make me gay?' I couldn't answer him. And I still can't."

We talked about the struggle in today's culture around an understanding of sexual orientation as a biological given or as a life style choice – and that struggle within the church, too. About the tension between the polarities in the culture, and in the church. About how those who are 'certain' of their posture (at either extreme) make it difficult for those in the middle who struggle.

I shared of my own struggle in the understanding of sexual orientation, of judging, of being led to the verses in the Sermon on the Mount when Jesus warns of the speck in your eye and the log in mine. Of my personal discomfort over the thought of male sexual acts, which is the log in my eye that colors my thinking. Of the nature of that special and 'complete love' which God desires and intends between two people. And in the end, of being led to the realization that I need to leave the 'judging thing' to God. But it hasn't made, and doesn't make, my own struggle easier.

I always carry my journal, a Bible, and a couple daily devotionals when I travel, so we pulled out the Bible and looked at the Sermon on the Mount. Ellen seemed to relax. "You know, I've known for only 2 months. But I've had a sense of it for a long time. The odd thing is, just a few weeks earlier I'd said to Steve that it wouldn't surprise me if someday Sean comes to us and tells us he is gay. He's very sensitive, is emotionally connected, and kind. He isn't effeminate. He had many, many girlfriends as best friends. He played sports all through high school and is talented in whatever he does.

"Even with Laura, though, I never thought he loved her. I never saw that passion that you see between a man and a woman. Yes, it was a deep, deep emotional love, and it still is. But that deep passion isn't there.

"And Sean has been so helpful in our struggle. One day he told us, 'I'm not a flamboyant gay – in fact, that behavior disgusts me. It's very personal. I don't even know another gay man. I've never been to a gay bar, and I don't have any desire to go to one.'"

The flight was ending, and so was our time together. As parting came nearer, I offered a suggestion that she and Steve seek out a faith community to help them on this part of their journey. Ellen smiled. "I've been thinking of that," she said. "In fact, Steve suggested maybe I should speak with someone because I'm struggling so."

"Well," I offered, "maybe it's something that would be helpful for both you and Steve to do together."

Ellen turned as she stood to gather her things. "Yes," she said slowly. "I've been thinking about that, too."

A story shared ... a blessing received.

Insights: *Shattered Dream*

The unexpected turn in Ellen's story took me by surprise. It is hard to imagine the emotion in the moment when Sean shared the news with his mom. At the time of our encounter several months after receiving his news, her voice quivered. But we'll come back to that moment.

What prompted her to reveal this deep intimacy of their family story, and to a stranger?

Perhaps revisiting her story as it unfolds holds a clue. Ellen had shared the 'safe' parts of her story – of growing up, of college and dating with Steve, of marriage and the family following. As the conversation turned to faith ("Ellen, tell me about faith. Has that been a part of your life?"), the story became more intimate. Both she and Steve had drifted from church over time. It wasn't intentional. That's just how their life unfolded ("…after we got married, we went to church a few times but it didn't become an important part of our lives.").

During *The Query* preceding the encounter with Ellen, stories of drift from church or faith no longer surprised me. However a story unfolded, the notebook simply captured what was being said. No commentary – neither affirmation, nor condemnation. Just listening and gathering. Her story continued: 'She sat silently for a few moments, and then asked about my faith experience.'

The storyteller had become the questioner. 'I shared of also being raised Lutheran, of marriage in the Catholic church but continuing in the Lutheran tradition, of being blessed with three children, in later years the painful journey of divorce … and all the while, a deepening faith.'

No doubt as my story unfolded, Ellen was moved that a stranger would feel comfortable in revealing such intimacies. Intimacies of the unraveling of a lengthy marriage, and intimacies of faith which carried him through. When my story concluded, 'She sat quietly.' It was in the quiet that she found the courage to share the depth of her *Shattered Dream*. What prompted her to ask about the role of faith in my life? I don't know. Perhaps it was in sharing of my vulnerabilities that she felt free to share hers. But the turn to a deeper level hinged on the shared story of faith. Trust emerged. Her shattered dream could have been the end of Ellen's recounting. But it didn't end there:

> "You know," she said, "Sean asked me a question a couple weeks ago and I couldn't answer it.

I felt so helpless. He asked, 'If God created each of us individually, and has a plan and a path for each of us, why did He make me gay?' I couldn't answer him. And I still can't."

We talked about the struggle in today's culture around an understanding of sexual orientation as a biological given or as a life style choice – and that struggle in the church, too. About the tension between the polarities in the culture, and in the church. About how those who are 'certain' of their posture (at either extreme) make it difficult for those in the middle who struggle.

I shared of my own struggle in the understanding of sexual orientation.

Ellen wanted to know my struggle, perhaps to help in her understanding. I shared that the struggle to gain clarity spanned several years and came to a head at a pivotal moment, and that to convey it fairly would take some time. She asked whether the remaining ninety minutes of the Chicago-bound flight would suffice, and we both chuckled. So, she listened attentively as my story unfolded:

With formative years on a Midwest farm and an engineering degree in hand, my corporate career began in Los Angeles, then the Bay Area, on to St. Louis, then to headquarters in Toledo. A shift in corporate strategy took me to the helm of a spinoff division with headquarters in eastern North Carolina. Eventually growing weary of corporate life, we chose to resettle to the central valley of California and put down roots. The roots grew deep in community, school, business, and church. In time, 'church' became more than just our home congregation. My faith journey followed paths of service in the polity of the denomination, including roles of volunteer lay leadership at state, regional, and national levels. For over a decade, the roles meant close interaction with clergy and lay leaders of a couple hundred churches in northern California and Nevada.

The diversity of California is both its intrigue and its challenge. That diversity encompasses many things, including social mores. Not surprisingly, tensions arise when regional identities and mores differ. As the decade of the 1990s unfolded, the 'bubbling up' of differing convictions around the matter of sexual identity and sexual orientation brought tension. In both the church and the larger culture, those tensions gathered steam. As a leader in the regional expression, my role brought innumerable opportunities to seek and encourage understanding in oft-heated debate among groups of differing and deeply held Biblical interpretation and conviction. In the strand of Lutheran tradition of which I was (and am) a part, tensions came to a head on the historic stance of the church which disallowed the ordination of a person in a committed same-gender relationship. Stridency in debate eclipsed civility. For me, the question of whether a gay or lesbian person could or should be ordained masked the core Biblical issue: are homosexual acts of sexual intimacy sinful? I.e., are such acts contrary to the will of God? Are they contrary to God's desired intent for humanity?

External tensions grew and my internal struggle deepened. In 1997, I was elected to the privilege of serving as a regional voting member to the denominational national assembly in Philadelphia. Such assemblies convene every 3 years, and matters of church practice and polity are considered. One morning, the breakfast hall was filled with round tables seating eight persons per table. A placard at each table identified the subject matter for breakfast conversation, thereby encouraging participants to select their subject of interest. I chose 'Breakfast with a Theologian'. Soon the table was full and the meal served. Idle pleasantries were shared. When eating had subsided, the gentleman seated beside me introduced himself as the theologian whose pedigree was described on the informational card. His credentials were impressive, including an endowed professorship at a prestigious theological seminary. To begin, he asked, "So, does anyone have a topic they would like to explore?"

The table fell silent; eyes glanced around. "No questions? Well, then our time together will be short because I have no prepared subject matter." The uncomfortable silence continued.

"Well, Dr. _____," I said. "I have a question, but the topic may be sensitive."

"No topic is too sensitive," he assured me. "What is your question?"

"The church is struggling with the question whether to ordain persons in committed same-sex relationships," I began, "but it seems to me, the foundational question in the debate is not being addressed. That is, from a theological perspective, is homosexual behavior a sin? I've pored over the Biblical texts, read many books and commentaries, and have tried to listen respectfully to the debate. But I'm having difficulty getting a clear understanding of the theology of the church on the foundational question. Is the act of sexual intimacy between two consenting adults of the same gender a sin?"

He was quiet as the question was posed, as were all around the table. Slowly and with respect, he began to articulate his understanding of the nature of homosexuality from a theological perspective and its Biblical basis. "And for these reasons and upon this foundation, we see that homosexual behavior is a sin," he concluded.

Relief at last! Someone of renown in the church with a definitive stance, and a rationale which could help me in my struggle.

Then he continued. "However, my esteemed colleague (as he nodded to the person across the table), the Reverend Dr. _____, has come to a different understanding." He cited his colleague's credentials and pedigree, of equal stature to his own, and invited him to speak, "Dr. _____, please share your understanding."

The second theologian did so, with equal conviction and equally persuasive theological argument based on solid Biblical foundation. "And so," he concluded, "we see that homosexual behavior is not, of itself, a sin."

Alas, 'Breakfast with a Theologian' did not bring clarity. But the experience brought a most meaningful insight. On this divisive matter, two highly acclaimed theologians within the same Christian tradition have been led to genuine and differing theological understandings of a Biblical 'truth'. Both are good, honorable persons. Though they disagree, both respect and honor the other. And in their disagreement, they are the church.

Several years passed. Within the church, the question of ordination became intermingled with the growing civil rights issues surrounding lesbian, gay, bisexual, and transgender persons. LGBT became the label of political correctness. Tensions continued to escalate within and among churches.

It was a Saturday morning. As a regional leader, I had been invited as part of a group to consider an appropriate disciplinary measure against a Bay Area church which had called a gay man to serve as their pastor. Discussion was respectful though strained. It was, for me, a difficult session. Through the years, I had come to know many in the room – but now, tensions were causing fractures in longstanding relations. I left deeply troubled.

After a fitful night, I arose early and settled at the dining table. Dawn was a couple hours away, the family asleep. Morning devotional materials lay before me. The readings for the day seemed empty. My relentless internal struggle over whether homosexual behavior is a sin was no longer a struggle. It was deep distress. "God," I prayed, "help me. I need your help. Help me." The intensity of my prayer matched my inner distress. I was in need of help. But from where?

Of course! "The Bible," I thought, "that's where God speaks." I reached for the Bible and prayed that God would guide me to the right words. Wherever it opened, I would read that section and find the help I was seeking. A good plan.

The Bible fell open at its center, in the middle of Psalm 119. I flipped to the beginning of the psalm, and quickly recalled that Psalm 119 is the longest of the one hundred fifty. Very long. But somewhere within, surely, the help I sought. I jumped in. It didn't take long for the reading to become a slog. By the time I reached verse 116, my mind was foggy. But that verse awakened me: *Sustain me, O Lord, as You have promised, that I might live. Do not let my hope be crushed.* I plodded on, but nothing. No insight to help me with the inner struggle.

> *Sustain me, O Lord, as You have promised. Do not let my hope be crushed.*

There had to be more. Somewhere in these words of God, there had to be more. I turned to the Sermon on the Mount, and began reading the words of Jesus. Matthew, chapter 5 ... nothing. Matthew, chapter 6 ... nothing. Matthew, chapter 7 ... verse 1: *Do not judge, so that you may not be judged.* Hmmmm ... no, nothing. Verse 3: *Why do you see the speck in your neighbor's eye, but do not notice the log in your own eye? Or how can you say to your neighbor, 'Let me take the speck out of your eye,' while the log is in your own eye? You hypocrite, first take the log out of your own eye, and then you will see clearly to take the speck out of your neighbor's eye.* (NRSV)

My reading stopped. ... *the log in your own eye* ...; ... *You hypocrite, first take the log out of your own eye, and then you will see clearly* ...; *Judge not, lest ye be judged.* (KJV)

The words would not leave me. Is homosexual behavior a sin? The log in my eye. Why has the reading stopped? God seems to be speaking to me, but what?

The log in my eye. It came to me, this log in my eye. For as long as I can remember, whenever the topic had come up of 'queer' or 'homo' (or 'gay' in more recent years), the image in my mind's eye has been of two men engaged in an intimate sexual act. Whether explicit or implicit in my upbringing and into my adulthood, that is to be regarded as an unnatural act. Suddenly, the log in my eye. It is the log by which my vision has long been impaired.

In the quiet of the predawn home, I sat stunned. The words of Jesus: *the log out of your own eye.*

Questions flooded over me, followed by near instantaneous answers:

Is it God's deep desire that we experience the 'complete love' God intends, between two people? Yes, it is.

Is it possible that God could bring a man and a woman together in the 'complete love' God desires in a faithful committed relationship, as a heterosexual union? Yes. Would such a heterosexual union be the will of God? Yes.

Is it possible that a man and a woman could be in a heterosexual relationship, but not within the 'complete love' God desires? Yes, that is possible. Would such a union be the will of God? No. Could a heterosexual act, then, be sinful? Yes, of course it could.

Could it be possible that two people, a man and a man, or a woman and a woman, be brought together by God and experience the 'complete love' God desires in a faithful committed relationship? Could it be possible that

God may bring two same-gender persons together for such a 'complete love'? Could that be within God's power or will? Could it be? Yes, if that were God's will, it could be.

Is it possible that a man and a man, or a woman and a woman, could be in a homosexual relationship, but not within the 'complete love' God desires? Yes, that is possible. Would such a union be the will of God? No. Could a homosexual act, then, be sinful? Yes, of course it could.

Is it possible for two people, whether heterosexual or homosexual, to be in a committed relationship and experience the 'complete love' God desires irrespective of sexual intimacy? Yes. Is such a 'complete love' dependent on intimate sexual acts? No. Must intimate sexual acts be the measure of the 'complete love' God desires? No.

Should I, then, be concerned with the level of sexual intimacy between two people (heterosexual or homosexual) who have found the 'complete love' of a God-desired relationship? No.

Is it, instead, the province of God to judge the presence of the 'complete love' between two persons? Yes. Can I leave that to God? Most assuredly, yes. Not only can I, but I must leave that to God. It is God's province to decide, not mine. It is not for me to judge whether the relationship between two people meets God's muster.

At that moment of realization, an indescribable peace flooded over me. My inner struggle and inner distress, whether homosexual behavior is a sin, left. It has not returned.

Ellen had listened attentively. As her story continued, she seemed to be at peace. Perhaps sharing my struggle had helped her with hers. Had my lengthy story helped in her distress? I don't know. But it is my story.

A Common Basis

"Jesus answered, "The first is, 'Hear, O Israel: The Lord our God, the Lord is one; you shall love the Lord your God with all your heart, and with all your soul, and with all your mind, and with all your strength.' The second is this, 'You shall love your neighbor as yourself.' There is no other commandment greater than these.""
Mark 12:29-31 (NRSV)

They were a young family of four with dad in the lead as they slowly worked their way down the aisle. The routine plea for volunteers to give up seats due to overbooking brought no takers. So, the plane would be full, not uncommon on direct flights from coast to coast. Both mom and dad were craning their necks as they peered ahead, assessing how their family might be split in pairs for the long flight.

Dad took the aisle seat and daughter the middle, while from the window seat I watched as they stowed their things. Mom and son settled in the row behind, so the family was reasonably together.

He was slender, of medium height with fine features and a trimmed mustache. Their dark complexion and dark hair suggested a family of south Asian heritage, perhaps Indian or Pakistani. The kids were quiet and well behaved, dutifully following the parents' bidding.

Dad nodded with a smile and a warm 'Good morning' as he buckled her in. She was about eight or so and as soon as he was settled, her head found his shoulder and her eyes closed. This would be a quiet flight, and a young girl in the next seat would mean a little extra room. Perhaps the long flight wouldn't seem so long after all.

Once airborne, he loosened her seat belt to let her snuggle into the seat and sleep. It was as though she were a half-grown kitten curled on a sunlit window ledge. The smile on my face brought one to his.

"Hi, my name is Larry," I said, as the smile continued. "Is she your daughter?"

"Yes. We've been traveling a while, so she'll probably sleep most of the way. My name is Kamal." His English was precise, but even so I asked him if he might spell his name as often I better understand how to pronounce a name unfamiliar to me after I've written it down. With pen in hand and the margin of the newspaper at the ready, he smiled and continued slowly, "K – A – M – A – L ... pronounced *kah-mahl'*."

"Kah-mahl," I repeated. It was an unusual name to me. "You've been traveling," I continued. "Where is home?"

"We're from Zambia and we're going to Seattle to be with their grandparents, my wife's parents, for 2 weeks."

"Zambia! Boy, you *have* been traveling for a while. How long have you lived in Zambia?"

"I was born there in 1971," Kamal replied. "Bateen, my wife, was born in the Fiji Islands in 1976. And this is my daughter, Bente," nodding to the little one curled in the seat between us. "She is 8, and my son is 10. They're excited to see their grandparents."

He told of their home in Kitwe, the capital of Zambia. The city has a population of about a million and is surrounded by copper mines. Mining is the major industry, and English is the primary language.

His father emigrated from India to Zambia in the 1950s. At the time, the Indian economy was in shambles and they had no money. His dad (Kamal's grandfather) had died. So, to survive, he and his brother worked hard to save and decided to move to Africa and start a new life. When they arrived in Kitwe, they opened a small grocery with an attached restaurant. Today, the family business also includes a restaurant supply house with sixty employees. In addition to the original restaurant and neighborhood grocery, they serve the metropolitan restaurant industry by wholesaling food, furniture, and commercial cooking equipment.

"Kamal," I interrupted. "Excuse me, but I'm intrigued by your story and I'd like to make a few notes." He listened intently to the premise of *The Query* project, and graciously continued while note-taking ensued.

Kamal is the baby of the family, with an older brother and two sisters. In 1992 at age 16, he decided to move to the United States to go to college. With an uncle in the Northwest, he picked a nearby university and earned a bachelor's degree in information systems. He landed with an IT firm in the area, and then another. The burst of the dot.com bubble in 2001 left him unemployed. By then, his brother had also moved to the U.S. and both found themselves looking for work. So, in 2003, they started an independent 'bargain dollar' store. But with high rents and thin margins, the skyrocketing price of oil sent plastic prices through the roof and margins shrank even more. After three years, they closed the business.

Kamal returned to Zambia to manage the family business. Today, with their dad in his eighties, he and his brother co-manage the business. "When I returned to Zambia, copper was $3-4,000/ton. Today it's $8,000/ton, so the economy is good now."

I asked him to compare life in Zambia with his memory of the 16 years he lived in the U.S.

"Life in Zambia in 1992 was very different from what it is today. But even so, in the United States as in any developed country, you take a lot of things for granted. The lights will always come on when you throw the switch. Things are always available in the shops. If you call 911, you get a quick response for police or medical emergencies.

"In Zambia, there are lots of electrical outages. Water from the tap isn't reliable and when it does come, it isn't always pure. Personal security is a constant worry. We don't have very good medical facilities."

He and Bateen have been thinking about returning to the U.S. so the kids can get a good education. "There just aren't qualified teachers or adequate resources in Zambia," he noted.

On the flip side, though, he noted that "when you're in New York or in Seattle, you're just another number and no one knows you. In developing countries like Zambia, the towns are smaller so everyone knows everyone. And that makes families closer together."

In Kitwe with its one million population, the majority are mine workers in the lower economic and social class. The average annual income of the working class is US$10-15,000. The impact of AIDS is real. In Zambia, the average life expectancy of the lower class is in the 40s or 50s, contrasted with the upper class in the 70s or 80s.

The middle or upper class is a small community. Kamal's family is among the upper class with an income about US$85,000. He and Bateen own their one-story home. It is on a big yard, with five bedrooms and a garden in front and back. "It's worth about US$150-200,000."

"The rising price of copper the last few years has brought big changes. Lots of Chinese are moving into Zambia, which is both good and bad. The difference is that in the 1950's, the Indians came in as family units and small business startups were the result. Those small businesses provided local jobs.

"But the Chinese are coming over in big numbers. Big organizations are buying out the larger mines, and they're not necessarily abiding by the laws of the country. They don't have humanitarian values compared to us. In business, their values are not our values. For example, we have all Zambian employees, all locals. The Chinese fill all their positions with Chinese, and so are taking away jobs from the locals. This trend has been underway for ten years or so, not just in Zambia but across Africa.

"China's hunger for commodities like iron and copper is driving them to Africa. They are acquiring them at whatever cost, even bringing prisoners from China to work the mines. They work, sleep, and live deep underground. Because they live in the mines, you don't see them. So, the mining jobs available to the locals are less and less as more and more mines are bought by the Chinese. We see it because we supply equipment to the mines and sometimes must make deliveries to the kitchens down below. So, we see what is happening.

"The mining industry has a lot of government regulations. There are certain jobs that are not to be filled with foreigners to provide jobs for the locals. For example, a wheelbarrow worker. But they bribe all the government officials. They 'grease the palms' to avoid the regulations."

I held up my hand for a pause. The story was fascinating, and it seemed the pen just couldn't move fast enough. I stopped for a moment and reflected on his story.

"You know, Kamal," I continued, "this kind of sounds like the Ugly American of the 1950s when the footprint of corporate America took hold internationally after WW II."

"Oh, no," he was quick to reply, "it's not the same at all. Americans have always had value for the human being. The Chinese have no value for human beings."

The words came with quiet conviction, underscored by his experiences in a part of the world unknown to me. He watched as I wrote in silence and then laid aside the pen and reflected. His words had caught me short. Maybe it was the seeming contrast between his serene demeanor and the certainty of his assertion which startled me.

"So Kamal," it was time, *"what is the reason for the hope that is within you?"*

The quiet conviction returned as his eyes held mine. "You just have to move on," he began. "Whatever life brings you, you have to move on as everybody else does. You do your part to support yourself, your family, and everybody around you – to play your part in life.

"My dad had a hardship in India, so he moved to Zambia. And when things were difficult in Zambia, my brother and I moved to the States. My family's story is the story of migration, a drive toward a better life. And that is where my hope rests. Whatever comes your way, you must keep driving toward a better life, wherever that takes you."

A pause. I continued, "To what extent, Kamal, has faith played a part in shaping your outlook?"

He pondered. Then, "Togetherness. From the beginning, our family has always been together."

I waited for more. Only silence. Kamal smiled and then caught me off guard: "Larry, what gives you hope?"

In this journey of *The Query*, he has been the only person to pose the question in return. I smiled, too, and shared that the reason for hope in me is grounded in my following of Jesus Christ – in the Christian understanding of the grace-filled nature of God – which gives me deep inner peace. His follow up questions were polite and respectful.

"We all have the same faith," Kamal continued. "It all has the same basis in a Supreme Being, and that basis is love. That's what keeps me with my family, to work together and to live your life. We are Hindu. Thus, the concept of Supreme Being. In Hinduism, we learn and we keep learning. There is still much I do not know. There is still much I have to learn."

The announcement, *'Please return your seats and tray tables to ...',* signaled our time together would soon end.

"I'm thinking about life as you have described it in Zambia, Kamal, and about the common basis we share in love. I wonder if perhaps the Chinese share that same basis, the basis of love, and that their value for human life rests there, too?"

"No," said Kamal, and the quiet conviction returned. "They do not believe in a Supreme Being. Love at the core is absent."

Perhaps, indeed, love is the common basis of humanity. But for Kamal, in some, 'love at the core is absent.'

Thoughts to ponder. The cross-country flight had not been so long after all.

A story shared ... a blessing received.

Insights: *A Common Basis*

Kamal's story was different from others in *The Query* because of the cultural setting where he lives. His life has been largely shaped in a part of the world with which I have no firsthand experience. Business interests have taken me around much of the globe, but not to Africa. His story was fascinating.

The story of his father, and him and his brother's, centers on overcoming hardship. His reason for hope, he answered, rests in perseverance, in driving toward a better life. Since to that point in his telling there had been no mention of faith, I broached it.

A pause. I continued, "To what extent, Kamal, has faith played a part in shaping your outlook?"

He pondered. Then, "Togetherness. From the beginning, our family has always been together."

Silence followed. It wasn't oppressive or uncomfortable. It simply was.

I waited for more. Only silence. Kamal smiled, and then caught me off guard: "Larry, what gives you hope?"

This storyteller had become more than 'the questioner'. This storyteller had posed *the* question. The one question which had prompted this entire undertaking. The question I most feared. No, Kamal's question wasn't verbatim to the 1 Peter verse: *what is the reason for the hope that is within you?* But it was close enough: *what gives you hope?*

For a moment, I considered dodging the question, of dodging the discomfort. There were any number of easy ways out which flitted through my mind: "My children give me hope," or "My grandson gives me hope," or "Laughter gives me hope," or maybe, even, "People like you give me hope." Any of those answers would have sufficed. Surely Kamal would have acknowledged with a polite smile and our brief time remaining would have been filled with other things – and all would have been okay. But it was my turn. The storyteller, now the gentle and respectful questioner. My turn to share the reason for the hope that is within me.

There had been no hint of Kamal's faith foundation. His story and the earlier answer to the query offered none. But in that moment, his faith foundation became irrelevant to my answer. And, in fact, my response was lengthier than the brief paragraph related earlier.

There is a school of thought in some Christian circles that a true believer must always be prepared with an 'elevator speech'. Such thinking holds that effective evangelism means a 15-second pitch always at the ready, so that even encountering someone between floors on an elevator presents an opportunity to 'witness'. But that thinking has always troubled me. Knowing me, were I on the receiving end of such an 'elevator' pitch, my reaction would likely not be very understanding. To my thinking, this 'God mystery' is far beyond a practiced sound bite.

In the 1980's, many churches began experimenting with alternative styles of worship. 'Contemporary worship' became the buzz phrase. My church, too, felt the nudge to explore a style which might find appeal to a changing demography. With the prospect of change afoot, a task force was duly appointed (of which I was a part) to study the issue and make recommendation. During one of the exploratory sessions, I suggested that creating an alternative style should include a fresh look at the language of 'church speak', i.e., the propensity of churches to use phrases which have historic significance but are unfamiliar in contemporary usage. "Give me an example," said Pastor Ron, the respected senior pastor. He was steeped in the historic liturgical tradition of Lutheran worship.

"Well, for example," I offered gingerly, "we always say the Apostles' Creed as part of worship. To anybody who grew up in church in a liturgical tradition, that's fine. But it doesn't mean anything to somebody who comes from a different tradition, or from no tradition at all. *Conceived by the Holy Spirit, born of the Virgin Mary, suffered under Pontius Pilate* ...that's all church gobbledygook. We need to come up with something that uses language people can understand."

Pastor Ron was quiet. "Ok, Larry," he said. "Write something for us to take a look at. Write a creed that we could use."

I don't know whether Pastor Ron realized what he asked, or the effect it would have on me. But that assignment proved to be one of the most significant influences in my developing faith. I was forced to examine the 'truths' of a faith I had inherited – truths which I had sadly never seriously contemplated. For the first time, articulating the 'God mystery' was before me. What are the truths about God that I believe? Unwavering, solid-as-a-rock believe?

In the end, I found that some of the historic expressions fit after all. The nature of God as 'trinity', a three-fold expression of God. Yes, to me God is beyond complete human understanding. But I claim solid belief in this three-fold expression:

<u>I Believe</u>

I believe that God created me and all that exists. [1]

I believe that as Jesus, God lived among us ...

> that Jesus shows me how to live my life today
> and learn God's will for me ...
> that by his death and resurrection,
> sin and death have been overcome ...
> and that I am a child of God forever
> because of God's great love for me.

I believe that as the Holy Spirit, God is always at work in my life ...
that the Spirit strengthens me through the community of believers
and that the Spirit works in the world through me
and through those around me.

My hesitation in replying to Kamal's question – *Larry, what gives you hope?* – was momentary. I began by explaining that an answer to that question, for me, begins with how I have come to understand the mystery of God. That my understanding is shaped by a Christian view of God, and in particular, the three-fold expression of God. From memory, I recounted my 'I Believe' statement.

"Because God's love is so great," I concluded, "I know that no matter how off track I get in my life, no matter how awful or unintended something I might say or do – no matter – God loves me, accepts me, and claims me. And the certainty of that unending, undeserved love floods me with a powerful inner peace, a 'peace that passes all understanding'. Every moment of every day that inner peace fills me, and I know it is of God. That unconditional love, and the complete inner peace it brings, is the reason for my hope. Even more, it is the certainty of my hope."

Maybe the *Brief Encounters* of *The Query* had prepared me, or maybe from just listening to so many stories. More likely, *The Query* had helped me realize that articulating the reason for hope within is deeply embedded and deeply personal. Even so, grandson Ethan would be proud: Turns out, it wasn't scary after all.

Kamal had listened quietly, thoughtfully, respectfully. In sharing his story – and now, mine – a blessing received.

Footnote:

[1] From the explanation of the 1st article of the Creed in the *Small Catechism*, by Martin Luther.

Brokenness

*"For by grace you have been saved through faith,
and this is not your own doing; it is the gift of God –
not the result of works, so that no one may boast."*
Ephesians 2:8-9 (NRSV)

Weather delays up and down the east coast from a winter storm meant a two-hour delay of this flight. There were hundreds of people sprawled at Dulles International relating stories of delay after delay, canceled flight after canceled flight. It was going to be a long night.

I had grabbed what looked to be an entertaining book to read on the five-hour flight (John Grisham, *Skipping Christmas*) and was looking forward to settling in to a quiet, enjoyable read. On the connecting flight, I had been digesting a used paperback, *The Confessions of St. Augustine*, and needed something to lighten the load and the journey. No 'query' on this flight. Just quiet, self-absorbed time alone.

He settled into the middle seat with a long sigh. A tall man, about my height, build and age. "Long day?" I asked.

"Yes, very," he replied. "I'm finally on this flight after waiting 10 hours. Two earlier flights to California were canceled. So, it's been a long day." The English was precise; the accent, clear.

Is California your home?

"Yes," he replied. "And you?" Yes, I nodded.

Where are you coming home from?

"I have been in Johannesburg for the last 3 weeks. So, on top of that long flight, a ten-hour delay here, and now 5 hours to California ... well, it has been a long day."

"Oh boy, you're going to want to sleep!"

He chuckled. "Yes, if I can. But I don't sleep well on airplanes."

The precise English and distinctive accent prompted my question as to his native tongue.

"Italian, but I speak several languages."

Why a visit in South Africa?

"I worked there for 40 years and was transferred to California 5 years ago. So, I went back to spend a few weeks as part of a celebration with some friends. It was fun to be back, but I'm looking forward to getting home."

And of course, my hopes for a quiet, self-absorbed flight flew out the window. With such a unique perspective, surely his story would be interesting.

We were airborne. I reached for my backpack under the forward seat, retrieved the notebook and *The Query* card, and ratcheted up the courage to engage despite his weariness. If he preferred a quiet ride, I'd find out soon enough.

"I'm intrigued by the little bit you've shared and imagine that you're probably dead tired and would like to be left alone. But before we get too far, I wonder whether you might be open to something? I'm in the middle of what I think is becoming a project leading to a book, and it means talking with complete strangers. So, if you don't mind, here's my card. I'm Larry. Let me explain."

"Hello, Larry. My name is Ignacio," as he returned the handshake and paused to study the card. "Hmmmm, risenindeed.com," he read the domain name aloud with a quizzical look. "That's an interesting e-mail address."

"Yes," I smiled. "I came up with that a few years ago, but you're the first person to say anything about it!"

"So, what is *'the Query … a book project'*?" he asked as he studied the card.

I fell into my now-routine patter. That for some time I've been reading a book, a compilation of writings by different authors. That one of them had used a phrase which has stuck with me, *always be prepared to answer the question whenever anyone asks of the reason for the hope that is within you, and do so with gentleness and respect…*

I paused before continuing to explain how his story might become part of *The Query*, but his reaction interrupted the pause. "Ah yes, Peter," he smiled. "From 1st Peter, as I recall."

I was surprised! This was a first!!

"That's right! I'm amazed you would know that! Are you a Christian?"

"Yes," he chuckled. "I'm a priest." We both chuckled.

And so was launched an engaging culmination of an otherwise dreary day. The time flew by.

"Well," I began, "normally I first try to learn about someone's life and then get to the query, and eventually explain where the query comes from. But you've already taken us to that piece, so let's start with the query and come back to your life story. So, *what is the reason for the hope that is within you?*"

If there was a delay, it was momentary – very momentary.

"The hope which I've been developing in my life is the message of the Gospel of Christ. What Christ was, is, said – is Truth. He is the only One who knows about life, truth – the reason for our existence. He is the full manifestation of the full plan of life – what we are for, what we are headed to.

"More and more, I see that Christ is the reason for hope. We must hook our life on something which gives meaning for good. To me, this is Christ. Christ gives meaning to everything."

We talked about Peter, his letters, and my conjecture that clearly Peter couldn't have written this, as the 'gentleness and respect' part didn't seem to jive with the bold, 'out there' Peter portrayed in the four gospels. He laughed, and concurred that it was probably written, as some scholars suggest, by a disciple of Peter.

Ignacio grew up in Italy, in Trent (yes, of 'Council of Trent' fame), one of seven siblings with three brothers and three sisters. His dad was in banking. The family was devoutly Catholic.

At age 12, he began having thoughts of entering the priesthood. He was ordained at 26 in South Africa and devoted 30 years there, followed by 10 years in Botswana. Five years ago, he was sent to the United States.

Ignacio belongs to a congregation of Stigmatines, one of many global 'religious congregations' in the Catholic church which have developed through the centuries. Stigmatines derive their name from the five crucifixion wounds, or stigmata (in Greek), of Jesus. While continuing in that tradition, he also serves a local parish as one of two priests. The parish consists of seven hundred families, where 60% are of Mexican descent. There are three services on Sunday, two in Spanish and one in English. In addition to his native Italian, he is fluent in English and Spanish which helps in administering the Sacraments and preaching and teaching the Word of God.

When he became a priest, Ignacio took vows of poverty, chastity, and obedience. So, he leads a life consecrated to sharing with others in the same vocation, "which gives my life meaning and direction."

Our conversation meandered delightfully. He was curious of my background in the faith (a Christian out of the Lutheran tradition), and we compared our understanding of Martin Luther's efforts to reform the church. He was remarkably well versed on the detail of the Reformation, kind in his comments toward Luther and in acknowledging that Luther's faith formation was rooted in Catholicism.

The dialogue was refreshing, acknowledging and honoring the faith practices of two Christian traditions separated by a schism reaching back over five hundred years. I couldn't resist and pulled from my backpack the tattered copy of St. Augustine's confessions, which prompted a look of surprise. "You're a lay person, a Lutheran, and you're reading Augustine? How refreshing!" he grinned. We laughed.

It has been my experience that folks within the Lutheran tradition are quick to proclaim (or claim) Luther as the great purveyor of 'justification by grace through faith' as central to Christian doctrine. Yet it seems to me that

Augustine of Hippo was the early champion for that thinking, centuries before Luther came along. "Yes, of course," Ignacio agreed, "but after St. Paul." Again, we chuckled, inasmuch as Augustine and Luther both cited Paul's writings.

Conversation turned to Holy Communion, the nature of the presence of Christ in the bread and wine, and the current reality of the inability to receive the Eucharist were either of us to worship at the other's church.

"The Eucharist is the essential nature of the 'oneness' of the church as the Body of Christ. Unless or until all Christendom embraces it in its fullness as understood by Catholicism, there can be no sharing of the table because to do so would be contrary to the foundational nature of the Eucharist as the Oneness in Christ.

"It is not sufficient to believe that Christ's body is *in* the bread. Rather, once consecrated, it is no longer bread. It *is* Christ's body, Christ's blood. It is no longer bread or wine. Those who do not embrace this teaching lack a complete understanding."

Therein rests one of the saddest aspects of the brokenness of the Church. Because as a non-Catholic I am deemed to lack a complete understanding of the Eucharist, I am denied the meal in Ignacio's church. And while Ignacio would be welcome and invited to receive Holy Communion in my tradition, he would refuse to participate because of the Catholic conviction that the sacred meal shared in churches outside the Catholic tradition is not fully understood. As a devout Catholic he would, therefore, deem it improper to participate. Ignacio's tone was thoughtful, his words declarative yet not judgmental. We acknowledged personal sadness over this divide, this brokenness, a remaining remnant of the Reformational schism.

For a number of years, one of my regular resources for devotional practice has been *Magnificat*[1], the daily Mass of the Catholic Church in America. "The daily meditations are often quite inspirational, "I shared, "though at times I wince at what seems to me to be occasional excesses in the veneration of saints or the adulation of Mary." Ignatio was thoughtful as he shared how meaningful those practices have been in his deep embrace of the Christian faith.

{By way of explanation, *Magnificat* relies upon *The New American Bible* for scriptural texts.

The *Apostolic Blessing* of Pope Paul VI on September 18, 1970, included these introductory comments about the new translation: *"For the faithful in all English-speaking countries the publication of The New American Bible represents a notable achievement. Its pages contain a new Catholic version of the Bible in English, along with illustrations and explanations that facilitate the understanding of the text."* (The New American Bible, World Catholic Press, a Division of Catholic Book Publishing Corp., Totowa NJ ©1987)}

I related my perplexity over occasional new-to-me phrases in *The New American Bible* and how the change in phraseology can introduce a meaning which seems far different from other translations. Ignacio acknowledged that he, too, lifts an eyebrow now and then over an unfamiliar phrase, and that he counsels the New Revised Standard Version as the most reliable English translation. "But," he asked, "are there particular verses that trouble you?"

Since earlier we had shared parts of our family histories, he knew of my marriage in the Catholic church, of being blessed with three children and two grandchildren, and of the painful ending of that marriage in divorce after 32 years. One of my deepest struggles during the time of separation and divorce (and to a lesser degree, a continuing struggle) concerned Jesus' teachings on divorce. We examined Matthew 5:32 and 19:9 where, in this Catholic translation, the words of Jesus make no mention of divorce due to adultery, marital unfaithfulness, or immorality. Instead, his words are in parentheses, *'(unless the marriage is unlawful)'*. We explored the significance of this change in phraseology and whether it may form the rationale for annulment in Catholic practice.

Ignacio was thoughtful. He turned to his digital pocket resource and called up comparisons of contemporary translations (e.g., this *New American Bible*, the *New International Version*, the *New Revised Standard Version*, the *King James Version*), then Latin, and then the original Greek. He studied the Greek at length.

"This is quite interesting," he began. "It is making me see the text in a way I had not considered before. The Greek seems to focus on a word, which the closest I can think of in English would be 'impure', as perhaps noting when the union of marriage is 'impure'. It seems that all other English translations have been in the context of an 'impure' sexual act within the marriage union, as for example adultery, fornication, prostitution.

"So," he wondered aloud, "because Jesus is talking about marriage and divorce, and not a sexual act, it seems this Catholic translation interprets the Greek text to mean the 'union' of marriage. Thus, if the union itself is impure', as in the union being 'illegitimate' or 'unlawful', that may be the basis of this interpretation of the original Greek. It would seem to hinge on how one translates into English this Greek expression."

Perhaps so, I noted, but to write the phrase *'(unless the marriage is unlawful)'* within Jesus' words as a parenthetical phrase seems peculiar. "Yes," he agreed. "It is strange, even to my understanding of the English language. I will give this more thought."

Ignacio was curious to learn more of my journey in faith. His questions were respectful, his insights compassionate.

A story shared ... a blessing received.

[Note from the author: Ignacio expressed delight months later upon receiving the original draft of his story. Along with some clarifying comments, he shared that he now is under new assignment in Rome.]

To: Larry Moeller
From: Ignacio
Subject: Re About 'the Query'
Date Sent: Thu 2/13/2014

Larry,

I have some time now to jot down some notes in the line you have asked me in your last e-mail - before I fly to the Philippines.

1. I like the spirit and style that you have chosen for your "Queries". One

feels the "extemporarity" of them (... I like to use neologisms...) which draws the interest of the reader for the spontaneity of the stories.

2. I like, now to say something about my experience in South Africa and Botswana.

I went to South Africa with another companion as a missionary (in Jan 1965), when we were asked (as theology students in the Verona's Stigmatine seminary) to join the group of older missionaries who founded that Mission in the Pretoria area in 1960 [they were previously in China, from where they had been expelled by Mao]. We completed our studies and were ordained priests there.

My motivation was to go and witness my faith in an environment where the heaviness of a traditional European Christianity should be less complicated. I was aware that I had to shed much of my structured Christian Catholic views of life, in favor of a more genuine and spontaneous Faith. I must admit that I did not arm myself with a thorough knowledge of the socio-political situation of South African history. The Apartheid situation was a shock which took quite some time to get me somehow "adapted" to it.

After my ordination I lived in our Religious community of Italian missionaries, right in the middle of the "black areas". This was an exception against the Apartheid rule of separation of blacks-whites, due to a traditional "permit", not written but tacitly agreed upon. That made us accepted and loved by the population.

The contrasts and challenges were however happening at the order of the day: when you move to places, enter shops, sit at a restaurant table etc. But one "adapts" himself to the system, and "survives"...with some scratches. In the middle of the 70's we were caught in the midst of the violence following the rebellion of the students in Soweto, which spread as "veldt fire".

Strange or "providentially" we survived with not much discomfort. Always protected somehow by that bond that we kept with the Africans with whom we continued to live. They somehow protected us. An interesting experience was to hear from our African friends an expression addressed to us the missionaries - when some dramatic happening of violence and racial killing had happened - and the hatred against the "whites" became more evident, - "but you are not "whites" you are priests" - answering our expression: "but we are also whites"!

In that context I realized and appreciated the great power of endurance and steadfast faith that support the common African, and in particular the Christian faith and solidarity that keep together those peoples.

Apart from the more active and courageous militant individuals who risked and lost their lives in fighting physically for the change of that society, the "common" people persevered humbly and hopefully - expecting to embrace the "redemption". And it did come.

Thanks especially to Mandela's enlightened vision and great heart, there was no revenge, except in the way of the "Reconciliation" and re-harmonization that he instituted. A true African miracle, that became an unheard of phenomenon that taught the whole of Africa and the world!

I was super-happy and proud to belong to that experience. I had become a South African citizen by then and I went to cast my vote when the time came, for the new government. It was truly moving to see the mixed queues of voters - black and white - smiling to one another and patient without tension. The transformation was very evident.

In living in Africa I might have lost the "advancement" and transformation of Europe, during those 40 years, - and in fact when I went back to Italy for vacations I did feel a bit out of place... - but I thank God that I experienced a way of life and a philosophy of life much more "human" and candid than the often sophisticated and artificial and "non-involved" European way of life.

The numerous groups of "volunteers", who visited us along those years and often stayed with us for some longer periods, sharing the African way of life and offering their service in various social and educational activities, have often said that they had experienced a deeper humanity, and bonds of love were strengthened forever.

I could speak endlessly of the way our African people live out their faith in the religious practices, and liturgical celebrations: joy, enthusiasm and spontaneity. People who live their humanity more spontaneously can experience the nearness of God and the power of the faith more vividly.

I went to Africa to look for a more genuine Humanity and Faith, and I found it.

Dear Larry, sorry for the long monologue, but I thank you for having given me the opportunity to voice it out.

God bless.

Fr Ignacio

Insights: *Brokenness*

Joy and sadness. The encounter with Ignacio was by far the most enjoyable in *The Query* experience and, for me, the saddest.

His reply to the question of the reason for the hope within him was beautiful:

> "The hope which I've been developing in my life is the message of the gospel of Christ. What Christ was, is, said – is Truth. He is the only One who knows about life, truth – the reason for our existence. He is the full manifestation of the full plan of life – what we are for, what we are headed to.

There was no time to rehearse content or cadence. No time to reflect:

> "More and more, I see that Christ is the reason for hope. We have to hook our life on something which gives meaning for good. To me, this is Christ."

Ignacio's answer was sincere and spontaneous, grounded in conviction:

> "Christ gives meaning to everything."

Threads of sincerity and spontaneity were woven throughout the conversation. It was as though we were brothers. He was intrigued to learn of my business experience, both in the corporate world and as a small business owner, and the intersection of faith and work in my life. He was enthralled with my first-hand insights of the inner workings of church polity at the regional and national level.

He was curious about life as a parishioner in the local congregation. He was even more intrigued upon learning of my recent experience. About three years earlier, I had been appointed by the regional church body to serve under special assignment as a 'licensed lay minister and mission developer' for a once thriving but now struggling small inner city church. Doing so had opened my eyes to the sacred privilege experienced by clergy, of meeting people at their most vulnerable in moments of deep personal loss or pain. Being attentive to the pastoral needs of a worship community and, together with them, learning to re-engage in a changing neighborhood deepened my faith. And all the while, juggling the demands of a small business. It had richly blessed me.

Ignacio probed techniques for walking neighborhoods and engaging the stranger. He lamented that the demands of a large parish had superseded his deep longing to be immersed in the surrounding village.

Many months had passed by the time the encounter had been transcribed from notebook to story. My e-inquiry for a physical mailing address brought Ignacio's prompt reply with his new station in Rome. Soon he had received the airmailed manuscript and our e-conversation continued. He expressed regret that during our flight, he had shared little of his experience of African life. My invitation to do so by e-mail brought delight and added insight as his story unfolded further.

There is joy in the encounter with Ignacio. And sadness.

My deep sadness rests in the brokenness of God's church, a brokenness of human making. Surely it grieves the heart of God.

We separate ourselves from one another over differences on if, when, how, or whether bread into body or wine into blood. My soul aches, knowing that the church – you and me – inserts its dogma between the hungry and God's most sacred invitation: the unfettered and unconditional invitation to the life-giving body and blood of Jesus in the bread and the wine of the Eucharist.

Thus says the Lord: "Let whoever is thirsty come to Me and drink. Streams of living water will flow from within the one who believes in Me." [1]

God alone knows if, when, how, or whether the Spirit acts upon the heart of a believer, new or old, so that streams of living water flow. Perhaps it may be through Holy Communion that someone first experiences this Living Water. But we have become self-appointed gatekeepers to the meal.

Long after the encounter with Ignacio, a prayer of invitation came to mind penned by a dear friend and fellow sojourner in the Christian faith, a sojourner in the Catholic tradition. It is a paraphrase of the opening lyrics to the title song by Robin Mark in his CD, *'Come Heal this Land'* [2] and expresses the sentiment that the invitation to the meal extends to all:

> *Let the exiled come. Let the weary come. Let the stranger come. Come and find rest, all you precious homeless ones. For a table awaits you, here in this house, where there is a place, a place set for you. So please come, come and sit at your place. Come, come and rest at your place. Come, come and eat, consuming God's grace. Come, come and drink, tasting God's mercy. Whatever your trouble, whatever your burden, please, just come, come to the table, come to the place set here for you.*

Sadly, the 'rite of belonging' at the table as instituted by Jesus has been eclipsed by the 'right of membership' in a church of human construct.

Surely, God grieves.

Footnotes:

[1] A paraphrase of John 7:37-38 as the Communion Antiphon for Friday, October 31, 2014, from *Magnificat*, PO Box 822, Yonkers, NY 10702. www.magnificat.com Tel.: 1-866-273-5215

[2] *'Come Heal This Land'*, original lyrics and music by Robin Mark. © 2001 Integrity's Hosanna! Music, c/o Integrity Music, Inc., 1000 Cody Road, Mobile AL 36695.

Epilogue I: *Reflections*

*"Fan into flame the gift of God that is within you ...
for you have been given a Spirit not of timidity,
but of power and of love and of self-control."*
2 Timothy 1:6-7 (a paraphrase)

It is not possible to express completely the depth of *The Query* experience. Revisiting the notebook brought me back to each interaction. Each moved me in its own way. Words on the page of a book cannot capture the richness of each story. Yet some things rise above others.

Gentleness and respect. Always answer the query with gentleness and respect, the writer of the I Peter letter encourages. Perhaps in those days the behavior of believers was so noticeably different as to prompt the question, *what is the reason for the hope within you?* Perhaps a life filled with hope was rare. Or perhaps the tone of the query would be one of derision, so that gentleness and respect would stand in contrast to the nature of the one asking the question. I don't know.

When gentleness and respect are extended, gentleness and respect are returned. Whether answering or asking, gentleness and respect returned.

At the outset of *The Query* journey, trepidation was my companion. Fear of ridicule or rejection.

Gentleness and respect trumps trepidation. Not once was the invitation declined. Not once, ridicule or rejection. In every instance, respect extended and gentleness received. In every instance.

How powerful in its simplicity, this encouragement: *with gentleness and respect.*

Listening. Do each of us carry a deep yearning within to tell our story?

Todd, the bankruptcy attorney and attentive husband in 'Everything Changed', spoke a sad truth as Kris's story concluded: *I've been reflecting that we don't really take the time to listen to people anymore.*

Perhaps the command to 'love your neighbor as yourself' begins with listening. Can we begin to demonstrate genuine concern for the other unless we know the depth of their story?

Years ago I was given an evangelism resource, long since lost. I can't recall the name of the booklet or the publisher, but one image in the shape of a triangle, and its perspective, has shaped my personal striving ever since:

That if I tend, first, to the relationship between God and me; and second, to the relationship between you and me ... God will tend to the third.

```
        God

    //      \\

  Me   ==   You
```

We get in trouble when I try to tell you what your relationship with God should be. God, through the Holy Spirit, will take care of that. When God provides the **Me == You** opportunity, conversations around each relationship arises, in gentleness and respect.

The journey of *The Query* has brought, front and center, the importance of listening as the '**Me == You**' relationship unfolds.

I wonder. How would a faith community – a church, a mosque, a synagogue, a temple – be perceived differently if it became known above all as *the people who listen*, and not *the people who preach*?

Authenticity. Skepticism abounds in the culture. It was present at the outset in most query interactions. The card helped. But it was the notebook which conveyed authenticity. With those more skeptical, the act of quickly flipping through page after page of scribbled notes dispelled the skepticism. Gentleness and respect, extended authentically, trumps skepticism.

Surrender. "*Fan into flame* ...", Paul admonishes his young protégé, Timothy. The gift of God within is, indeed, a spirit of power, and of love, and of self-control.

There is some comfort, I suppose, that Timothy needs to be reminded that the gift within him is not a gift of timidity. If Timothy was finding it difficult to be bold in the Spirit, then there is hope for me.

Surrendering to the deep compelling which prompted *The Query* meant embracing this gift of power ... of love ... of self-control. Had timidity prevailed, as it has far too often in my living, there would have been no Query. No stories shared. No blessings received. And I would have been the poorer.

"Fan into flame the gift of God that is within you ... "

To God alone the glory.

Epilogue II: *A Movement*

The Premise
*Always be prepared to give the answer to the question when someone asks
of the reason for the hope that is within you ... and do so with gentleness and respect.*
(1 Peter 3:15)

The Deep Compelling
*Quit worrying about how you are going to answer the question. I want you to ask it.
No, not sometime. Today. On this flight. Now.*
(Journal Entry)

The Challenge
I wonder. How would a faith community –
a church, a mosque, a synagogue, a temple –
be perceived differently if it became known above all
as *the people who listen*, and not *the people who preach*?
(Epilogue I: *Reflections*)

What if *The Query* was more than a collection of stories? What if, instead, *The Query* became the impetus for a cultural course correction? What if, through *The Query*, we became serious practitioners of 'love your neighbor as yourself' through intentional listening to that neighbor? What if *The Query* became a movement – an authentic, one-on-one, neighbor-to-neighbor movement? And what if the common thread of such a movement was a query of hope, of hope within? What if the foundation for such a movement was as simple as listening to stories of hope?

What might be the consequence of such a movement?

It would be beyond our imagining. A groundswell of one-on-one encouragement. *Encourage one another, and build each other up*, indeed! What might be the consequence? God knows. God alone knows. God already knows.

How could such a movement begin?

It already has. And it is gaining momentum, one by one. And now, with you. One by one.

Is this your Deep Compelling? To ask the question, and listen – listen to stories of hope? And by listening, give and receive encouragement? Amazing how God works. Through the Deep Compelling, God is restating the Premise, to *always be prepared to ask the question. and do so with gentleness and respect.*

Or maybe this is your Deep Compelling – *I want you to ask it. No, not sometime. Beginning now. Today.*

Enlist others in church or workplace, civic group or school, newspaper or nonprofit, business or Chamber of Commerce. Gather stories throughout neighborhoods. With the help of the local newspaper, publish them - e.g., *Stories of Hope: Maryville, Tennessee.*

Imagine the impact, for example, of nonprofits in your community gathering and publishing stories of hope from the recipients of their services.

Are you ready to be blessed beyond imagining?

Getting started

A simple prayer:

> *God, I don't know what You have in mind, but I know You want me to do this. I'm putting my trust in You, and surrendering to the Deep Compelling. Help me. Amen."*

If you haven't already, find a copy of *The Query*. If it's yours, mark it up, jot notes in the margins. Underline phrases that are meaningful to you.

Make a personal commitment to engage in twelve query encounters

Confide in someone you trust of your commitment. Ask them to check in with you occasionally. If they embrace the concept of a Higher Power, ask them to pray for you.

Buy a notebook or journal. Make your own calling cards through a local office supply store, perhaps something like:

The Query ...
stories of hope

Your Name
Your Address
Your Town, ST 12345

youremail@yourprovider.com   (123) 456-7890

Find a light but durable tote bag or knapsack to hold pens, calling cards, your notebook, and your copy of *The Query*. You may want to include a travel Bible and a favorite devotional. Begin carrying the bag everywhere, because you will be surprised when opportunities surface unexpectedly.

Send an email to me, Larry Moeller ... querier@risenindeed.com ... and say something like – *Larry, I get the Deep Compelling of the Query, and I'm stepping up. So I'm going to listen more than preach. I will make at least twelve queries and gather the stories, and decide after that whether to continue. Pray for me.*

Watch for settings where quiet conversations of 30 minutes or more make sense. In time, you will experience delight when they pop up: at lunch cafés or coffee houses; in customer lounges at car dealerships or oil change shops; in waiting rooms for jury duty; on subways or trains; during airport layovers, or on flights. You will be surprised when opportunities arise, often in places and with persons least expected.

Query #1 ... **step by step**

In a setting with potential, a simple prayer:

Surprise me, God. Open my eyes to see who is before me. Amen.

Aha! Someone alone. Take a deep breath.

Ok, God, I'm surrendering. I'm trusting You to help me. Bless what is about to happen. Amen.

Approach, with gentleness and respect.

Hi ... pardon me. My name is _____ (give the calling card; let him/her study it for a moment*). "I'm working on something ... well, it's actually a project about listening, and I'm just getting started. It's fascinating, and it works best with somebody I don't know. Can I take a minute to explain it?*

Listen ... then continue.

Ok, thanks. Again, my name is _____ (extend your hand, to shake hands). *Who am I talking with?*

Let me explain. I've been reading a book, called The Query. In it, the author relates the stories of complete strangers and their answer to the same question. And the question is: 'What is the reason for the hope that is within you?' The stories are fascinating, and all across the board.

So The Query is a project about listening, and about hope. I'm fascinated by the whole idea, and am collecting stories about the place of hope in people's lives. So, to begin, tell me a little about you ... your family and your early years ... and we'll see where your story takes us. I'm going to make notes (show the notebook), *because my memory isn't what it used to be. And this way, I can remember your story. At some point I'll ask about hope. But let's start with where you were born, and a little about your parents and your growing up years.*

Remember, you are just listening – gathering a most precious story, the story of a person's life. Let the story unfold naturally, following the thread wherever it leads. Ask about siblings, about grandparents, about school, or friends, or jobs, or hobbies. Ask questions for clarity, gently and with respect. Occasionally, read back a note you've made, to make sure you've been listening well.

Once the story has come to the present, say, *I'm going to pause for a moment and review my notes ... so give me a moment, please.* Use this time to clarify. Then, continue with the query: *You have had a remarkable life. Now, let's go to the query. As you reflect on your life, 'what is the reason for the hope that is within you?'*

Capture the words precisely as spoken. Don't be afraid to ask for time to let note-taking catch up. Gathering the reasons for hope is the centerpiece of *The Query* experience.

Let any further conversation unfold naturally, making notes as appropriate. To bring the conversation to a close, perhaps use something like –

Thank you so much, _____. This has been very special. I wonder whether you'd be open to sharing your contact information, in case I want to get back in touch with you? I'm not sure what the future holds for this project, but I'd like to be able to get back to you if appropriate. An e-mail address or phone number would help. What shall I use?

If possible, gather full name, phone number, e-mail address, and physical mailing address.

Congratulations! You have successfully navigated Query #1!

How do you feel? Were you nervous? I'd like to listen as you share the experience. Please reach out to me by e-mail ... Larry Moeller ... querier@risenindeed.com. In the subject field of the e-mail, write *After Query #1*, and then offer your insights around these questions:

1. What have you learned about yourself, through this experience?
2. Describe the setting.
3. What is the person's first name? Describe him or her in twenty words or less.
4. What was the most positive aspect of this experience?
5. What was the most difficult?
6. What will you do differently in Query #2?

Query #2 through Query #6 ... more steps.

Revisit the steps for Query #1. Make adjustments to fit your style and personality. Remember that authenticity is important, as important as gentleness and respect.

Decide whether you wish to learn about the role of faith in the storyteller's life, especially if faith has not been introduced before or during the answer about hope. Maybe that will come after several Queries, as confidence builds. Or maybe it is an aspect of *The Query* which is too discomforting for you, and you decide not to probe about faith. Either way is okay.

In my experience, exploring the aspect of faith brought a rich and deepened understanding. But approaching it can be very delicate. As a number of the stories in *The Query* attest, many people have turned away from religion, from church, from faith, from God, because of harm or hurt. If the topic of faith has not surfaced in the story up to and through the answer about hope, it is probably because of a past harm or hurt. So, approaching the matter of faith can be delicate.

Maybe part of **Epilogue I: *Reflections*** merits another look:

"Perhaps the command to 'love your neighbor as yourself' begins with listening. Can we begin to demonstrate genuine concern for the other unless we know the depth of their story?

"Years ago, I was given an evangelism resource ... long since lost. I can't recall the name of the booklet or the publisher. But one image in the shape of a triangle, and its perspective, has shaped my personal striving ever since:

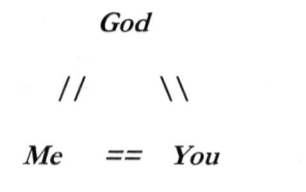

"That if I tend, first, to the relationship between God and me; and second, to the relationship between you and me ... God will tend to the third.

"I get in trouble when I try to tell you what your relationship with God should be. God, through the Holy Spirit, will take care of that. When God provides the opportunity, conversations around each relationship arises ... in gentleness and respect.

"*The Query* journey has brought, front and center, the importance of listening as the **Me == *You*** relationship unfolds."

When God provides the opportunity. Perhaps this *Query* experience is just that opportunity. An opportunity to build trust, and to listen. Just listen.

A cautionary note. If your motivation for undertaking *The Query* is to evangelize – to tell the Good News; to save the lost; to invite someone to church – then I would discourage you. Don't. Why not, you might wonder?

Back to **Epilogue I:** *Reflections* –

"I wonder. How would a faith community – a church, a mosque, a synagogue, a temple – be perceived differently if it became known above all as *the people who listen*, and not *the people who preach*?"

This project, *The Query*, is about listening … with gentleness and respect. First and foremost: listening.

But if with sincerity and authenticity you do wish to learn about the role of faith in the storyteller's life, how would you proceed? My approach was simple and genuine, and effective. After recording the answer to the query … *what is the reason for the hope that is within you?* … you might continue like this:

Thank you. Thanks for sharing your story. It has been fascinating. And now, _____, I'm wondering about something, so let me dig a little deeper and if it is uncomfortable for you, that's okay. You don't have to answer. I'm wondering about 'faith'. What part has 'faith' played in your life? To what extent has faith been a part of what has shaped you?

Now, let silence enter. Give the person as much time as he or she needs to think about a response. Keep in mind that your role is to listen. Simply to listen, and not to suggest an answer. Just listen, and gather the story. You will be richly blessed.

Be sensitive, and careful to avoid commentary on the answer you hear. There are no wrong answers to your follow up question about faith. So be careful to avoid 'teaching' or 'preaching'. You are simply the listener.

Bringing the conversation to a close can be the same –

Thank you so much, _____. This has been very special. I wonder whether you'd be open to sharing your contact information, in case I want to get back in touch with you?

I'm not sure what the future holds for this project ... but I'd like to be able to get back to you if appropriate. An e-mail address or phone number would help. What shall I use?

If possible, gather full name, phone number, e-mail address, and physical mailing address. Then, if you feel comfortable and it fits the context of what has been shared –

Oh by the way, _____, there's an interesting piece to all of this. The author of The Query didn't come up with the question about hope. That comes from a verse in the Bible, from 1 Peter 3:15. It says, "Always be prepared to give the answer to the question when somebody asks, of the reason for the hope that is within you ... and do so with gentleness and respect."

Thanks for sharing. It has been a privilege to listen.

After completing Query #6, pause to reflect. You are no longer the novice. Perhaps you've added your own touches to technique. Once again, please reach out to me by e-mail ... Larry Moeller ... querier@risenindeed.com. In the subject field of the e-mail, write *After Query #6*, and then offer your insights around these questions:

1. What more have you learned about yourself, having now experienced six *Query* encounters?
2. What has been the most positive aspect of *The Query* project so far?
3. What has been the most difficult? Why?
4. What changes in technique have you tried? Which worked, and which didn't? What changes would you recommend to others?

Query #7 through Query #12 ... more.

With six query encounters under your belt, the uncertainties and butterflies have diminished. Not disappeared, but diminished. Confidence has grown, and so has enjoyment. You are being enriched by the stories with which you are being entrusted.

In Queries #7 through #12, your technique will continue to be refined. Perhaps you will experience the thrill of faith in their lives, or feel their pain. By the conclusion of Query #12, your technique will be so routine that it has become second nature. You have developed an easy and confident approach to a stranger. You have learned that by listening to his or her story, unexpected blessings unfold.

And so, one more time please. Reach out to me again by e-mail ... Larry Moeller ... querier@risenindeed.com. In the subject field of the e-mail, write *After Query #12* and share while I listen:

1. How has *The Query* experience changed you?
2. Does there seem to be a common thread in the stories you have gathered? What is it?
3. If you were starting over, what would you do differently at the outset of *Query #1*? Why?
4. Finally, what changes in technique would you recommend to others?

Beyond *Query #12*

A story shared ... a blessing received.

Every *Query*, a **Me == You** blessing.

A dozen queries have prepared you for the joy of more. How many queries are in your future?

How many blessings can you endure? How many blessings will others receive because you listened?

The Challenge
I wonder. How would a faith community –
a church, a mosque, a synagogue, a temple –
be perceived differently if it became known above all
as *the people who listen*, and not *the people who preach*?

Step up to the challenge, as together we strive to be *people who listen*, and not *people who preach*.

Welcome to the Movement!

Appendix: *Study Resource*

The stories comprising *The Query* offer opportunities for learning and reflection. Small discussion groups of four to seven participants are particularly effective.

Stories of Hope

Select a facilitator within the group and decide how many stories to tackle in each session. Develop questions which fit your context. They may include:
1. Does the opening quotation fit the story? Why, or why not?
2. Describe the character in twenty words or less.
3. What is the reason for her/his hope?
4. To what extent has hope been important in their living?
5. If you could ask one question of this person, what would it be?
6. What have you learned about yourself, from this story?

Insights

After discussing the stories in each section, turn to the **Insights** for that section and discuss:
1. What insights by the author do you share? Why?
2. With which insights do you disagree? Why?
3. What other insights have you gleaned from the stories?
   a. About the character(s)
   b. About the author
   c. About you

Epilogue I: *Reflections*

The author offers reflections on his experience gathering the stories for *The Query* into four general areas. What reflections would you add? Why?

Gentleness and respect

    a. The writer of 1 Peter 3:15 encourages gentleness and respect when answering the question about hope. Why?
    b. Are gentleness and respect necessary when asking the question? Why, or why not?
    c. In your life experiences, when have gentleness and respect helped in dealing with a difficult situation?
    d. When would a difficult outcome have been different if you had extended gentleness and respect?

Listening

The author uses a three-sided illustration to describe relationships with God, with neighbor, and between God and neighbor.

    a. Do you agree with the descriptions? Why, or why not?
    b. When is listening more effective than preaching? When is preaching more effective than listening?
    c. Do others perceive your faith community as *people who listen*, or *people who preach*?
    d. How could you change, to become more welcoming? How could your faith community change?

Authenticity

    a. Do you agree that 'skepticism abounds in the culture'? Why, or why not?
    b. What are some characteristics of authenticity?
    c. How do you know when someone is being authentic? What instincts do you trust in assessing authenticity?
    d. When someone engages you in a conversation of faith, are you skeptical of their motive? Why, or why not?
    e. In asking someone of the reason for their hope, how would you convey authenticity?

Surrender

In the introductory *Journal Entry*, the author characterizes a deep compelling as something which is "so foreign and brings such extreme discomfort that it marks the certainty as a life shift ahead." He confesses at **Insights: *A***

Deep Compelling that "surrendering to the *Deep Compelling* flies in the face of who and what I am. It is, for me, the most difficult."

    a. Is a Deep Compelling different from a matter of conscience? Why, or why not?
    b. What are the consequences of deciding a matter of conscience?
    c. What are the consequences of surrendering to a Deep Compelling?
    d. What are the things that inhibit us from surrendering to the Deep Compelling?
    e. Describe a Deep Compelling in your life. Did you surrender to it? Why, or why not?

Epilogue II: *A Movement*

Name some movements in human history which began with one or two people. Who were the people? How long did it take to gain momentum?

Some movements are for good; some are not. What movements for good are underway today?

The author suggests that one-on-one encounters modeled after *The Query* can affect a 'cultural course correction'. What do you think the author means, by 'cultural course correction'? Do you agree? Why, or why not?

As this 'listening' movement grows, imagine the changes ahead. Share and discuss.

What could you or your group do today, tomorrow, next week, to launch *The Query*: to listen and gather stories of hope?

Consider the suggestions in Epilogue 2: *A Movement* -

- Work with Chambers of Commerce, newspapers, faith communities, etc. to gather stories throughout the town or city and publish them, e.g., *Stories of Hope: Maryville, Tennessee*

- Imagine nonprofits gathering and publishing stories of hope from the recipients of their services.

Acknowledgements

Janet Ward, the first to hear the story of Quentin. Her quiet and steady encouragement kept *The Query* project before me when distractions arose and enthusiasm lagged. Thank you, Janet.

Brian Malison, for the gentle nudges prompting me to share how the journey of *The Query* was changing me. Thank you, Pastor.

Pat Hunsberger, for clarifying questions and an eagle eye in editing the first draft. Thank you, Pat.

The many executives in industry, so quick to say 'yes' to voicing their impressions of the early draft – and their occasional queries during business about progress of *The Query*. Thanks to so very many!

The adult Sunday school class of St. Paul Lutheran Church in Maryville TN which devoted several weeks in 2014 discussing the stories. Their thoughtful conversation brought insight to the potential of *The Query* as a study resource. Thanks, all!

Debbie Lehman, whose gift of a heavily-edited second draft helped tremendously. Thank you, Debbie.

Frank Couch, whose suggestions over lunch altered the shape of *The Query* – from a collection of short stories, to a book. Thank you, Frank.

Bonnie Anders, whose objective insights to the fourth draft brought further refinement. Thank you, Bonnie.

To each person whose story comprises *The Query*. Thank you, for changing my life.

Above all, to God – the Mystery of the Ages – who discomforts me so. Thanks be to You.

About the Author

*"Grampa likes to go fishing with me, but we don't catch very many.
And when we're camping and its real dark and we're in the tent, he tells scary stories!
And he likes to roast hot dogs and cook beans over the campfire,
but he doesn't like pineapple.
And he likes to hunt dragons with me, and watch Star Wars.
And, oh yeah – he likes to take long walks and watch me ride my bike!"*
Ethan

With an engineering degree from Iowa State University in hand, Larry Moeller entered the corporate world. Twenty years later, he co-founded and owns Libarty Group. Libarty is a premiere executive search firm serving Client companies across North America. It specializes in helping companies fulfill their mission by identifying, attracting, and retaining exceptional talent.

Working hours find him and his colleagues embedded in a delightfully restored 1920's office space overlooking the Smoky Mountains from downtown Maryville, Tennessee. With a home in nearby Knoxville, Larry and Deanna enjoy their blended family of a daughter, four sons, and four grandsons.

He is the author of *Claim the Flame*, a series of seven two-character dialogues featuring the apostle Paul and his 1st century church contemporaries. © 2015 Larry D. Moeller. Parson's Porch Books, publisher.

www.ingramcontent.com/pod-product-compliance
Lightning Source LLC
Chambersburg PA
CBHW071826110526
44591CB00011B/1240